❧ The Gift of Healing

The Gift of Healing

A PERSONAL STORY OF SPIRITUAL THERAPY

BY Ambrose A. Worrall
WITH Olga N. Worrall

1817

HARPER & ROW, PUBLISHERS
New York, Hagerstown, San Francisco, London

This book is dedicated to

our beloved Mothers

REBECCA BROWN MATTOCKS WORRALL

ELIZABETH MARY KARANCZAY RIPICH

❧ Contents

8 : CONTENTS

PART III: MEANINGS

ॐ Foreword

"You can approach the undying flame, but you can never touch it."

A friend of ours quoted this statement to my wife Olga and me long ago. We have never forgotten it. Our lives, indeed, have been in many ways a quest, a seeking to know and understand this flame.

Both of us are known as "sensitives"—persons subject in unusual degree to the influences of psychic forces, particularly, in our case, forces associated with spiritual healing. For almost half a century we have sought to use this healing power solely for the benefit of others. We know that no power exists in and of ourselves; we are merely the channel, the vehicle, for a power that is not ours to command.

In our work in spiritual therapy we neither seek nor do we accept payments or offerings of any kind. Nor will we accept patients who refuse to see a physician. Doctors and medicine itself are among the instruments of God's healing. Many physicians are our close friends. Many have sent individuals to us, in special cases.

We have, in our files, many letters from individuals telling us of healing they have received, letters written with warmth and love, a deep and real outpouring of gratitude.

Yet this gratitude does not truly belong to us. We ourselves are deeply grateful for the opportunity to play a role in healing, grateful to serve as its instrument. We seek neither personal glory nor profit.

The gifts of the spirit are often unrecognized or misunderstood.

One reason for writing this report on our healing ministry is our hope that others will be encouraged to carry on this work in their own lives, to explore and to seek to develop their own latent spiritual gifts and understanding.

For these gifts are within us in varying measure and can be developed to their full levels of power, so that our lives, both physical and spiritual, become more meaningful for ourselves and others in the demonstration of Divine healing power.

We are grateful to all who have assisted in the editing and gathering together of material, and to old friends and new who have given us permission to use their stories and letters in this record.

OLGA AND AMBROSE WORRALL

PART I ❧ SEARCH

1 &ə Vision

On the second floor of a large mid-Victorian home in a tree-lined residential district of Cleveland, Ohio, a twelve-year-old girl climbed out of bed in the darkness and quietly stepped into the hall. She tapped on her parents' bedroom door, then whispered, "Mama, there are people in my room again."

Olga could hear her father's words spoken in Hungarian to her mother: "Elizabeth—wake up! It's Olga. She sees them again. You'd better go to her."

The mother arose and hurried out to the young girl standing at the door. "Darling—Olguska"—she used a Russian term of endearment—"you know we've told you before—there is no one in the room. Nothing, no one. You only imagine . . ."

Her fingers smoothed the girl's long light hair. Back into the girl's bedroom she went. She turned on the light for a moment to show the youngster how empty were these strange imaginings. They had been going on for nine years—these visions the girl claimed to see. They were causing the mother and father increasing concern. Of all their children none except Olga had such strange aberrations.

Yet even with the light on, Olga kept insisting that it had been real, she had seen them. "I saw a woman with a light-colored dress standing beside the bed—just as real as you. The dress was bright yellow and it was very pretty and full. She had gold hair. She had a little white dog in her arms . . ."

She continued to babble on with more details about this woman she had seen, until the mother suddenly cried out that the description sounded like Juliska, a friend she had known as a girl herself in Hungary. "But how could you know, Olga? For Juliska lives in the old country, she doesn't live in America . . ."

"But she isn't alive," Olga declared firmly. "She told me she had died."

The mother looked into Olga's face intently, angry at hearing these dreadful words from her own child. "You must never, never say such things again, Olga," she commanded her daughter. "It is wicked. Do you understand?"

Obediently, the girl nodded. Whatever she had said must be wrong because her mother said it was wrong. Yet she *had* seen the lady in the yellow dress and heard her speak her words. It *was* as real as life. Of that Olga was absolutely certain.

The mother could only look at her daughter in bewilderment, wondering how she could help the girl to be rid of all these wild nightmarish imaginings. In every other way twelve-year-old Olga was a typical child, like all the others in this huge family, playing, arguing, laughing, talking too much, getting into too many cookie jars.

"I will stay here with you tonight," Olga's mother said gently. "So you won't have to be afraid."

She turned out the lights. In a few minutes mother and daughter were peacefully asleep, side by side, in the large hand-carved wooden double bed.

A week later a letter arrived from their relatives in Europe. "Things go well," the letter stated. "But there is a note of sadness. Our dearest Juliska—you remember lovely golden-haired Juliska—died suddenly only last week . . ."

Halfway across the world—in the city of Barrow-in-Furness, on the northwest coast of England—another child, six years old, called out in the darkness, "I can see them—I see people."

Around him in the room, glowing in the dark, it seemed, the

boy saw people, grownups and children. They were as real to him as any he saw in daylight on the street. Only they never spoke, these people, these children. Sometimes the children would seem to be playing together, wordlessly, noiselessly.

The six-year-old boy lying in that darkness, surrounded by these children others could not see, was myself, Ambrose Worrall, native of Barrow-in-Furness, born on January 18, 1899. But it had not occurred to me that other people did not see these adults and children in the darkness as I did. They had visited in my room many times before.

My father came into the room to calm me down. He was a large genial man who loved life and people and took things as they came. "It's only the bogeyman," he assured me, in a quiet half-joshing tone. "Now you watch out there, boy—or that bogeyman'll get you."

Except for my father's refusal to believe they really existed, the visitors did not bother me at all, the silent adults I saw, the children at their play. But this unseen bogeyman of whom father spoke filled me with sudden terror.

I was six years old and the bogeyman at that age had a frightening sound.

To me, these experiences, occurring at different times, in cities thousands of miles apart, present a remarkable parallel in the lives of Olga and myself: the "dead people" visiting her in her home in Cleveland, and my "visitors" in our house in the ancient seacoast town of Barrow-in-Furness. Years later, when the convolutions of chance—or destiny—brought Olga and me together across these thousands of miles, neither of us knew about the psychic experiences of the other. In fact, we were hesitant to speak of such things; we were very much attracted to each other, and like any other pair of young people, meeting in the early stages of young romance, we had no desire to startle or frighten the other by experiences we ourselves understood hardly at all.

Nor could Olga or I guess the unique psychic adventure we were to share together in our lives.

Our healing ministry we carry on quite apart from other aspects of our everyday lives. Olga runs our home and is interested in neighborhood and community activities. I have my work as a consultant to a major industrial aerospace corporation on the outskirts of Baltimore, a company with which I have been associated for more than forty years.

Yet it is our work in spiritual healing and our other interests in psychic investigation that give our lives meaning and purpose and destination. They have given us an outreach to the world, to many thousands in need, through individual cases that come to us, through our nightly time of healing prayer and meditation, through the New Life Healing Clinics in the Methodist church with which Olga has served for over fifteen years, and I also in a lesser measure. Our mail seeking help, or reporting progress or healing, mounts to perhaps a hundred letters a week, with the totals running over the years to perhaps a hundred thousand. They come from all over America, indeed from all over the world, with every conceivable approach and problem, some urgent and desperate, others seeking perhaps only a moment of consoling peace. A letter from a man we had never heard of before, on an island somewhere in the British West Indies: "I ask you to please pray for me . . . I wound up down here in a little island and my family and I have worked hard . . . I have not felt well for a long time. I neither have the time or money for a trip for medical attention but . . . I am a little lonely down here and ask you to join me in prayer for help. I will think of you all the time and ask you, please join me. Thanking you ever so much. . . ."

Most of the letters, the phone calls, and the visits are from average people, businessmen and businesswomen, homemakers, teachers—a whole cross-section of today's world and today's life.

Some are deeply religious, a few come quite skeptically, almost daring us to help them. Some come to us because all hope for help in any other direction has been written off. "I have nothing to lose but my life," one woman informed us during her interview. "And the doctors have told me there is no hope."

But the woman didn't lose her life.

This outreach that Olga and I have been privileged to share is the most rewarding experience we could ever have known.

But let me make clear at once my own attitude and approach. I have always favored the scientific approach to all phenomena. In spite of all I have seen and experienced in the field of healing and other psychic investigation, I seek to maintain an objective, open, and at times a skeptical point of view. I believe that all areas of human and spiritual activities should be subjected to the most exacting examination, precisely as I expect the stress calculations on the structure of a new aircraft to be examined down to the most exacting requirements. I believe we should employ, in our research into spiritual therapy, the latest and most applicable scientific methods to gather data that cannot be obtained by casual observation. We should seek, by the scientific approach, to understand, to learn the laws governing spiritual healing.

The quest here as elsewhere should be an open-minded search for truth about the eternal and unchanging laws of God and the universe. I believe that most so-called "miracles" are not miracles in any accepted sense, but only the working out of these immutable universal laws on a higher level of consciousness and being than we know.

Perhaps I can give you an example of how these laws work, in practice, in the case of a wonderful child named Kay.

Kay's father originally came to me about this case. I knew him as an important executive in a large Baltimore manufacturing company. He was deeply troubled. His daughter, Kay, six years old, was in a coma in Baltimore's Sydenham Hospital. She had been stricken with measles—an ordinary case of measles, everyone thought. But one day her mother had been unable to arouse the girl. Terrified, she called the doctor. When he arrived, he placed his hand under the girl's head and tried to lift it but could not. The girl was paralyzed, rigid from head to foot.

The physician at once ordered the girl be rushed to Sydenham Hospital, where her condition was diagnosed as encephalitis—sleeping sickness. (I am informed that there is less than one chance in five thousand of this kind of case developing out of measles, but it does happen.) At that time there was no medical cure or even treatment for this type of encephalitis that had any real value. The cases could be and often were fatal; where patients did recover, there was often severe brain damage and residual permanent paralysis.

Moreover, the records indicated that after a certain number of days of coma, death almost inevitably resulted, Kay, in a coma now for sixteen days, had passed that time already.

The father was himself distraught and desperate. The prolonged day-and-night suspense had brought him close to the breaking point. He knew of our work in spiritual healing. Since the doctors told him there was no more they could do, was there any way in which we could help?

Because of her contagious condition, no one was allowed to visit the little girl in the hospital. I agreed to treat Kay by the only method possible, absent treatment. The father gave me a picture of the girl from which I could work. That night, at home, with this picture before me and in my mind, I followed a technique I have developed of "tuning in," to become, in a metaphysical sense, one with the patient.

As I sat there, I felt this affinity almost immediately sweep through me. I put down the picture and turned off the light. I then felt a flow of healing force which comes often in such healing procedures from the solar plexus region of my body. In such moments, I am extraordinarily sensitive to all reactions and I was again almost immediately aware that this healing force was being opposed by an unusual barrier surrounding the child.

At the same time I saw before me in the darkness the face of the father. I could see that he was concentrating intensely on something. I did not know what it was. But I was sure that it had something to do with the force field effect I had been experiencing —the turning aside of the power. Why? The father above all wanted her well.

I called the father the following morning to discuss the case. I asked him directly, "Were you thinking about your daughter last night?"

The father said yes, he had been concentrating on his child, concentrating on the idea that the throat muscles of the girl—at least that much—could relax, so that the tube that they had put through her nostril for feeding purposes could be removed. I told him I did not think it was wise to concentrate on the girl's throat in that way. It would be far better, I said, to think of her as being in good health, as she was before her illness, to picture her in perfect health.

He agreed to co-operate. That evening I "tuned in" once more and this time felt no resistance to these healing waves which I felt flowing from me.

That night Kay opened her eyes for the first time in eighteen days. The fever subsided sharply at the same time, and the paralysis was cured as far down as her waist.

Within a few days the whole situation had been quite turned around. There was no longer danger of contagion and she could be brought home, the physician said. She still, however, was not again whole. She had only 10 per cent vision, and a plastic paralytic condition of the legs. None of these residual effects, the physician told the parents, could or would improve in any measurable degree.

Kay's physical condition did not improve in the next several weeks, and the father at last asked me to visit the girl at her home. I found her in bed, propped up by pillows, attempting to read a child's book printed in letters three fourths of an inch high. Even so, she was holding the book only about five inches from her eyes.

When I came in she put down the book and asked, "Are you my new doctor?"

I said, "No—I'm not a doctor. I've just come to visit you."

I went over, picked her up in my arms. I smiled at her. I tried to put her on her feet, gently, not to harm her, and her legs were without any sign of strength, sagging like the legs of a rag doll. I put her back into bed.

I sat down on a chair beside the bed and we talked. We discussed many things but not her trouble. All the time we talked, I kept asking myself, "What am I supposed to do?" I have learned over many years to wait for the intuition that I know will come.

After about fifteen minutes I felt impelled to put my hand on this little girl's back under her pajama top. For perhaps two to three minutes I rubbed her back. At last little Kay said, "My, that feels good." I continued the ministrations for a few minutes, then told her, "I must go now; it's getting late."

Kay wasn't having any of that. "No, you have to stay here," she insisted.

I told her I had to go home to sleep because I had to go to work in the morning at the Martin plant.

Urbanely, six-year-old Kay informed me, "You don't have to go home; you can sleep right here. There's plenty of room in this bed."

I explained that I had other things that required me at home, but assured her that I would come again. So she agreed to let me go.

The next morning the father dropped in to my office. He was smiling. He told me that when he went in that morning to carry Kay to the bathroom she said, "Daddy, I don't need you to carry me." And she got out of bed by herself and walked to the bathroom.

Little Kay fully recovered—she has no trace of the paralysis and has twenty-twenty vision. Years later, grown up, she wrote us about her career. She was working in a good job in an insurance company; she had many dates and her most important problem was deciding which one she would marry. "The next time I get to Baltimore," she wrote, "I hope to see both of you, on one condition, that you have a dish of candy on your coffee table . . ."

Often we do not hear of a healing until the individual writes to ask for help in some other direction. "Dear Mr. and Mrs. Ambrose," one letter begins, "I wrote you in 1960 for healing for my husband for which he received healing. I am so grateful to you. Thank God and may He bless you. Now I'm writing about my dad who has cancer in his right arm. I'm asking you to pray for him and his healing. . . ."

And so we pray.

We live in Baltimore, Maryland, in a charming yet unpretentious house, in a pleasant but certainly not in any sense extraordinary community, the Northwood section. We do not go into trances. We do not give readings for hire, we do not go in for showmanship, crystal balls, and trumpet seances. We are not performers. We will allow no commercialization of what Olga and I consider gifts that have been entrusted to us to be used for others.

I suspect that we do lead extraordinary lives in regard to the amount of hours and energy we pour into our varied and often sharply contrasting activities. Olga is an excellent housekeeper and an artist in the culinary department. In addition to managing the household and the meals, she also carries on her duties as director of the healing clinic of the Mt. Washington Methodist Church, conducting healing services, conferring with those seeking healing, handling all the correspondence not only at the clinic but also in our home. At our healing evenings in our home, held twice each week, Olga works with those who come, preparing them, talking with them, helping to ease their mind and emotions so that when I see them in the healing room—it is on the second floor of our home—they understand something of the approach and techniques employed. Olga was also a member of the local garden club but gave up this post when the demands of our work became simply too great. We are not rich, we have no secretarial staff; whatever we do, all the letters, all the answers, all the telephone calls, all the visits, we do ourselves.

Apart from all this I had my work for the Martin Company, a division of the Martin Marietta Corporation, formerly the Glenn L. Martin Company, whose Baltimore plant I helped to set up and launch into operation in 1929. There were seventy-five of us that formed the nucleus of the force in Baltimore and watched the number grow to over fifty thousand strong. I became involved in many duties in this company, from plant layout through design and building of tools, detail manufacturing and assembly and test operations. I was concerned with field service, estimating, negotiation of contracts, planning, liquidations, procurement, lecturing, surveys, evaluations of subcontractors' capabilities and performance, engineering design problems, cost control, cost reduction, and value engineering. My fields of activity included design and manufacture of aircraft, missiles, rockets, nuclear devices, vacuum chambers, electronic computers, and modules—even a dishwasher. My longest tenure of duty was as manager of the cost planning and estimating department which kept me busy for fifteen years, during which time we produced estimates covering approximately three billion dollars worth of production. Upon my retirement as an employee of the Martin Company in March, 1965, I signed a contract with the company to continue my association with them as independent contractor furnishing consulting and advisory services.

My education and occupation in the fields of aeronautical, mechanical, and electronic engineering, and production, together with my interest and work in research and development in these fields, and the need to produce tangible results in the way of profit and performance, have made me take the questioning approach and examine carefully every proposal, plan, every performance report. I am therefore skeptical by nature and training and follow a daily pattern not given to fantasy or self-deception.

In our healing work Olga and I report only what we have experienced; we admit, at once, that there is much that has happened to us, both individually and together, that we do not understand. We know that we are dealing in largely unexplored, little understood areas, spiritual arenas, psychic forces.

Interpretations that may be put upon these experiences vary according to an individual's concepts and levels of thinking. The way in which any healing takes place is mysterious, and none more so than in spiritual therapy. We do not know the actual mechanical and chemical agents and psychical reactions called into play. We believe this is the field we must investigate, not only in private groups and healing rooms, not only in our churches and prayer cells, but equally through the laboratory, the test tube, the miscroscope.

We have submitted to many tests, in some instances to try to measure the healing force that flows through the body, in my hands, for example, in the actual process of healing with the Biblical technique called the laying on of hands. In other instances Olga made tests involving speaking and answering questions regarding events of the future—speaking and responding to questions in one instance in languages she does not herself either speak or understand. We have provided data on some of our cases to Dr. J. B. Rhine of Duke University and to other study groups and investigators in extrasensory perception, psychometry, precognition, and related phenomena.

Significant also in spiritual therapy is the role of intuition, and what is called—often in scorn and derision—clairvoyance. These too appear to have a valid role, although they are avenues little understood and only beginning to be investigated on a scientific level in our colleges and universities.

In this area of precognition Olga appears to have particularly strong gifts of perception. There are times when this kind of pre-awareness involves bizarre and even melodramatic episodes.

One morning at breakfast Olga told me that she was literally quivering as the aftermath of a dream she had had. "I was walking down a hospital corridor," she related. "I heard a baby cry, and my concern was to find the baby. But as I neared the room where the baby was crying, I saw flames and smoke pouring out of the doorway."

So intensely real was all this in her mind that she almost seemed to forget, as she related the events, that they were only fragments of her dream. "Before I could get there, the crying stopped. I heard voices of men and women telling me not to go into the child's room. I could hear the words, 'Don't go in there, you can't do anything for the child. The child is dead, he's been destroyed in that fire.'"

These voices only seemed to make her more determined to rescue this baby. "I ran through the flames into the room, saw the infant lifeless in the crib, picked it up—it felt stiff in my arms—and ran through the burning doorway."

She ran down the hall, she recalled, trying to find another room for the infant. The voices of the men and women followed her, taunting her, "The child is dead. The fire killed him."

At last she found a room without fire. "Inside I lifted up the child, high above my head, and prayed to God, 'Please, dear Lord, heal this child, give him back his life.'

"When I finished that prayer," she said, "I felt the infant stir in my arms, open his eyes and look at me. The next instant I was awake."

That evening Olga and I were visiting a husband and wife whom I knew mostly from business and whom Olga was meeting in person for the first time. During the visit at their home my wife saw sitting on a sofa across the room the spirit of an elderly woman with an infant boy on her lap. Only Olga saw this, only she heard the woman declare that her name was Mamie, that she was the mother of the husband and that the sofa she was sitting on had been her bed when she lived on earth. And she was pleading with Olga to tell both the husband and the wife that she had the baby and that it was in perfect health.

Somewhat shaken by this, Olga wondered what the young couple would think if she heeded the request. How does one report such a thing in the midst of a normal social evening? But the urgency and importuning of the elderly form finally forced her to tell them what was happening. She described the woman named Mamie and the infant in her arms.

The wife cried out with great joy, "My baby, my baby—he's not burning in hell—he's alive. Thank God, thank God—you are giving me back my baby."

After the wife grew more calm, the husband told Olga, "You are entirely correct in this. My mother's name is Mamie. That sofa where you saw her—that was her day bed, on which she slept, in her apartment. She died several months ago.

"We had an infant who was to have been baptized at the age of six months. But when he was five months, he suffered a convulsion and died without benefit of baptism. A pastor at the services told us this child was conceived in sin, died in sin, and would eternally burn in hell."

Neither Olga nor I believe that any major denomination today subscribes to this interpretation of scripture. But coming as it did with the seeming support of the church, it brought untold additional agony to this young couple in their loss.

The message which the man's mother had sent them through Olga brought them a whole new wave of hope—and of life.

This woman ultimately became pregnant for a second time and the doctors told her that there was little chance of her carrying the child beyond the third month. Bleeding had started. The husband called me at once and I gave her spiritual treatment and the laying on of hands.

The bleeding stopped that night. She eventually gave birth to a completely healthy and normal child. The husband wrote us that November, "I can think of no more appropriate time to write this letter than this day of Thanksgiving. D. and I have so much to be thankful for that mere words are not adequate to express our undying gratitude to you both for making this the happiest Thanksgiving of our lives. . . ."

I recall one remark of the husband that first night we were with him. He turned to Olga and said, "You might have known my mother's name in some way, I suppose. But how could you have known that this was her couch, that it used to be in her apartment and I brought it here after her death?"

On the way home that night I reminded Olga of her dream-story. "The baby that they all said was dead," I said, "and the flames from which you took the infant. The fact that you saved the infant from the flames. Just as you did here tonight—in another way. You saved their child—for them—from the flames of hell."

Much that does happen we ourselves cannot explain. What occurs in our experience is like the unfoldment of a garden in spring, as great a mystery to us as the garden might be to a child walking its paths and discovering its beauty for the first time.

But to relate the unique adventure that has been our lives, we must begin with the first intimations and experiences of two children—Olga and me. Children and strangers, half a world apart.

2 ❧ Where No Man Stands

Barrow-in-Furness sits on the coast by the Irish Sea. Here was our home. Here for me was the beginning of meaning and impressions.

My father, Alexander Worrall, was employed for some years in the vast industrial complex known throughout the world as Vickers, Ltd., manufacturers of guns and ships, planes, cannons, and heavy machinery. Eventually he ran a stationery store where, as a boy, I helped out by delivering papers, waiting on customers, cleaning up the shop, opening up in the morning and sometimes helping to close up at night. Often I was up before daylight to get out-of-town papers at the railroad station, bring them, together with the local papers, to the store and later carry them to the gates of the Vickers plant where my father and I would sell them to workers on their way to the various departments. Then I would run all the way from the plant gates to my school, a distance of perhaps several miles. (I later became a long-distance runner in high school.)

My father was, in his own special way, a triumphant human being. Everyone loved him and he loved everyone, but he never made any real money, although we were always comfortable and never went hungry. What records he kept in the store were scanty at best; if someone came in to make a purchase and had no money to pay until Saturday, it was all right. Bring it in on Saturday. And if they forgot, that was all right. People would always pay him, sooner or later, he would say. He was born in Staffordshire, ran away from home as a boy, went to sea on great sailing ships, came home, and moved from job to job in various communities until he

27

settled down in Barrow-in-Furness. He was a Methodist but not unduly religious.

When he was in need, something would turn up. He used to tell us of a time as a boy when he was walking along a country road with a friend seeking employment in the next town when suddenly he said, "Wouldn't it be great if I found half a quid?" They were, at that time, without funds. Fifty yards farther along the "something" turned up: He picked up half a quid lying on the road.

He ran an insurance business on the side but never made any profit out of it; he was always carrying policies even after they should have been lapsed for nonpayment of premiums; he didn't have the heart to close out the policies, and often wound up having to meet the premiums out of his own pocket. He never prepared for tomorrow. It would take care of itself, he would say; and in some way or another it always did. He was a man of laughter; he loved a good story; he loved people and the world. My sisters and I had little tin banks in the house into which we put our weekly allowances and the tips I received from customers for delivering papers. My father insisted I share these tips with the girls, although it always seemed to me unfair because I did all the work.

Sometimes at night, when we children were asleep in bed, he would, with the aid of a kitchen knife inserted in the bank slot, slip out some of the coins. Of course we knew about it, but he did this only when he was short of ready cash. It was all right with all of us, because he always put the money back as soon as his temporarily impecunious circumstances improved.

He went to church, chiefly, I think, through my mother's resolute prodding. He had only slight interest, at best, in things psychic or sacredotal. Yet I recall one episode he related to us that he could never explain away to his own three-dimensional satisfaction.

At the plant a sling broke and a gun carriage fell from the

overhead crane and killed his brother, who had been working there also. Grieved and shocked by the tragedy, my father nevertheless accepted the grisly accident stoically.

One night, however, some weeks after the accident—my earth-bound, profoundly nonmystical father had a second jolting experience: A form appeared to him in the darkness of his bedroom, a figure he recognized as his own brother. The figure was distinct, there was no question that it was his brother. The apparition, however, did not communicate, speak, or give any indication of awareness that my father was there. The brother appeared to him several times, always in the same way, always without saying a word, always at night, always in the same room. Finally my father became angry at these visits, angry with himself as much as with this silent, wordless phantom. "One night when he appeared to me," my father told us, "I said to myself, I am going to find out who or what you are. Whereupon I got out of bed, ran across the room, and threw my arms around the figure. But my arms embraced nothing at all, only the air and darkness."

The apparition of his brother never returned after that.

In many ways my mother was the practical, stabilizing force in our home. She was very small, with long, lovely, curly auburn hair, so long and beautiful that other women were envious. She was born in Scotland. Her parents died when she was very young, and although she was supposed to have inherited money, all of it was used up by the time she was of age to receive it. She came from Scotland to Barrow-in-Furness, where she found employment. Then she met my father and they fell in love. The only special item about their romance (so far as I have been able to determine) was that they were married twice on the same day. The minister didn't arrive on time and some other qualified person there performed the ceremony in his stead. Just as the substitute minister was concluding with the words "I pronounce you man and wife," the real minister ran in, breathless and apologetic, to explain that he had been delayed unavoidably en route. But here he was, ready and able to officiate. So they obliged him by allowing themselves to be married twice on the same day.

The night I was born a friend ran to the Vickers plant to tell my father that mother was in labor; another man ran to get the doctor who lived even farther away than the Vickers plant. Transportation and telephonic communications were scanty to nonexistent in that part of England, even at the threshold of the new century. Neither my father nor the doctor arrived before me. I had one sister, Edith, two years older than I. Later I had other sisters, Rebecca and Barbara. A baby brother, my mother's last child, was stillborn.

Most of my early childhood was the typical childhood of any lad in this industrial community of Barrow, surrounded by the green hedgerows and rural beauty of Lancashire. We lived a normal, routine family life.

On Sundays, under the goading instances of our Scottish mother, we spent a great deal of time in church. I attended Sunday School in the morning and afternoon. This was followed by the regular church service both in the morning and later in the afternoon. There was, in addition, an evening service at six o'clock which we also attended when circumstances permitted.

Occasionally my parents, after the six o'clock service, would go to still another service, in another building in Barrow known as the Psychological Hall. On these evenings we children were taken home and put to bed. I cannot recall that we grumbled over not being allowed to go with them after a long day of sitting in those assorted pews, with time out only for meals.

One Sunday evening, for reasons I never discovered, I was taken with my parents to one of these Sunday night sessions at the Psychological Hall. This was a large brick structure. In the left corner, inside the hall itself, was a pipe organ and next to it a choir loft, in front of which was a rostrum. This was, I discovered many years later, a spiritualistic study group; there was no one on the rostrum; four or five apparent leaders sat in front of the rostrum, on the level of the front of the hall. The rest of those present, perhaps forty or fifty others, together with these leaders, formed a square, facing inward.

There were double rows of spectators sitting on the three sides of the square, facing the leaders. My parents and I were in the outer row. One of the leaders announced that we would start by singing a hymn. But there was no organist to play and no other instrumental accompaniment to the singing, and even to my untutored young ear it was very much off key; my father had a beautiful baritone voice, but he was only one of many. The hymn was followed by a prayer, the prayer by another hymn, and then men began to talk. With no idea of what this was all about, I began to look around the hall. As I did so, my attention was drawn to an elderly gentleman who stood near an office located on the right side of the hall, near the platform but on the level of the hall itself where we were seated.

I remember wondering why no one appeared concerned about this old man, and why he was not asked to join the rest of us in the group. A woman came over and spoke to someone in the row ahead of us, and this discussion distracted my attention from the man. When the conversation ended, I turned my eyes back to the office door; he was still there. I decided that he had come in uninvited and was waiting to be welcomed. I asked my father if I could go over and tell the old man that he could sit with us.

My father paid no attention whatsoever to me. After a moment I nudged him and again requested him to let me go to the man. He asked me what I was talking about. I pointed to where the old man was standing. "I want to invite that man to come and sit with us. He is old—he must be tired."

My father peered across the hall to where I pointed. He had excellent eyesight. He looked hard and long. Then he turned back and informed me, in unmistakable tones of annoyance, that he wanted to hear the speaker, that there was no old man standing by the office door, and would I please be quiet.

I could see the man, and I knew that my father, with his excellent eyesight, could not fail to see him also. I could not understand why my father would lie to me. I was so distressed about this that I kept hoping all through the meeting that I would have another opportunity to ask my father again. But when there was another break in the talks, I looked again to the spot and saw that the man was gone. I was sorry.

The episode was particularly significant in my life as an example of my own dawning realization that I was in some way different. I did not want to believe I was different; I did everything I could to deny it in my own mind. I brushed it aside. I was simply a boy like all other youngsters; I ran, I jumped, I played ball. I fought with my sisters.

Still, the awareness was there. I had learned, for example, not to speak of the people—the visitors—who came at night to my room. It was wiser, I found, not to talk of these things.

The old man was a little different in my mind because he was so real, because this was happening in the bright light, and because I knew he was there. I really believed my father had lied in insisting that he could not see this man.

I did not want to believe, here in this lighted hall with all of these people around us, that I was seeing in a way different from the way they saw.

Years afterward I was to visit that hall again, as a young man in my early twenties. I told one of the officials of this hall the story. I even described the man I saw. He seemed impressed by my description and asked me to follow him to another part of the building where I had not been before. There he pointed to a picture hanging on the wall along with some other photographs. "Is that the man you saw?" he asked.

The instant I saw the picture I realized that this was the man whose personality and face had made such an impression on me.

The official then said, "It's very interesting, because this man was the head of a spiritualist group who were active in this building for many years. But he died many years ago—I would say about ten years before you were born."

3 ❧ Apprenticeship

Another incident out of my very early boyhood occurred in Sunday School. I recall sitting in the class and listening to the teacher read to us, from the ninth chapter of the Book of St. John, the story of how Jesus anointed a blind man's eyes with clay and spittle, and how after the man, at the command of Jesus, washed off the clay and spittle, he could see.

That morning on my way to Sunday School I had seen a blind man on a doorstep only a few streets away. Why could we not get some mud and spittle and put it on this man's eyes and let him wash it off so that he, too, could see? To my young mind the idea seemed entirely logical, and I posed the question to my teacher and the class. The teacher was startled and perturbed. Unsure of his facts, he took refuge in the statement that only Jesus could do such things and that such miracles no longer could happen.

He informed the class that the healing of the blind man in the Bible took place two thousand years ago, that Jesus could heal in this way because He was the Son of God, that no one else is the Son of God and that no healings such as He accomplished could be done today.

I felt a wave of disappointment with this answer. Did not Jesus set the example to us—to do as He did? Why should God stop such healing after sending His Son to us to give us this example of His healing love. Was He not sent to show the way? Why should such healing be possible two thousand years ago but not today?

It made no sense.

Despite the psychic experience and episodes of my early youth, however, I had at that stage no concept of the role that healing

33

was to play in life, no hint of any of the unfolding patterns into which I was to be drawn.

I was, I believe, of a sympathetic nature toward others, and I was given an example of concern for others by my parents. Each week my mother would prepare buckets of soup to carry to the poor people who lived not too far from our home. I remember I had to carry the soup into a very impoverished section of our city, past lodging houses where drifters and tramps loitered in the doorways. The whole atmosphere was anything but reassuring, and I never tarried long en route to and from these soup-bearing missions. But they did help to make me sensible of the importance of helping others in need. This was a vital part of my young training: my mother's profoundly religious outreach to the community, a Christian love displayed not only within the walls of the church but equally beyond the walls. From my father I had the example of a strong, of perhaps more earthly compassion. He was brother to the world; the world was brother to him.

I recall one not atypical incident at my father's stationery store. My father sold tobacco there as a convenience for customers who picked up newspapers and cigarettes en route to work. The only reason he sold cigarettes at all was that the tobacconist shop next door didn't open in the morning until an hour after my father's shop. One day my father was having a new sign painted on our store and the painter, on his own initiative, painted the sign: "A. Worrall: Stationer and Tobacconist." The wording was accurate but, according to my father's code of doing business, it would be unkind and unfair to his neighbor, and he compelled the by then bewildered painter to paint out the word "tobacconist" immediately.

That was the kind of man he was. And that was the attitude, an example, I found in their lives, an example of obligation, even to a stranger, to go with him even the second mile.

Their teaching had its effect on my attitude in those growing-up years. Yet many of the other things that happened to me, the occasional episodes of psychic character, did not make a very deep impression upon me. I knew that certain things happened; on occasion I thought about them, wondered about them a little, but did not grasp for a moment how they might really affect my entire life. Certainly I had no idea that these were intimations of two worlds I would follow, one of the spirit, the other of science and industrial production. I was a boy growing up, a typical youngster with three sisters of various ages whom I loved and badgered almost as much as they badgered me.

The world, the modern world, was very much with us all.

At thirteen I was graduated from grammar school and scheduled to take what was known as a "labor examination" which would permit me to go to work full time in my father's store. But fate moved in. By chance I was delayed and unable to arrive in time to take this examination. Another would not be given for months. So I stayed at grammar school, taking advanced subjects to prepare myself more fully for high school, which I entered at the age of fourteen.

I was fortunately a good student and received top grades in my classes. I even won a nation-wide essay contest conducted on a national scale and participated in by thousands of high school students throughout England, Wales, and Scotland. The subject was "Bread." (I believe the sponsor was a bread company.) I won first prize.

I was also interested in mathematics and sciences, not merely in theory but in facts, in exact answers. Shortly before the age of fourteen, working with other students, I constructed a wood theodolite and surveyed and drew plans of the school playground. We also determined the height of the flagpole by trigonometrical methods.

These were the opening months of World War I. Munitions and armament plants, including Vickers, Ltd., were overwhelmed with war production orders. Trained manpower was scarce. I was engaged at Vickers as an indentured apprentice for training to become a fitter and turner. I continued my education in evening school. I was working at Vickers (the standard week was fifty-three hours). Most of the night school teachers during this period were also engaged in war work during the day. My apprenticeship started out as a five-year shop-training course. I worked in every department, helping to build howitzers and naval guns, turning out mechanical parts on drill presses and lathes, assembling fuel heating pipes, installing machinery, turbines, propeller shafts, thrust blocks, range finders, ammunition hoists, and other equipment, fitting them by hand in situations involving close tolerances and great exactitude. It was a working panoramic education in modern machinery, rigid airships, submarines, monitors, cruisers, battleships, engines, and engine rooms. At the same time I was going to high school and later to Barrow Technical School to complete my education. Here the subjects ranged from theoretical and applied mechanics to calculus and pure mathematics, including studies in stresses and strains in materials and structures, machine drawing and design, heat engines, laboratory work to prove out the theories and formulas for determining such things as the calorific value of coal, heat transfer, mechanical advantages, and other technical areas necessary to a thorough education in mechanical engineering.

I had little time for psychic episodes. Those few experiences of an extrasensory nature that did happen I dismissed or else I tried to find rational, naturalistic explanations for, in accordance with the physical laws I was learning in my work and my studies at night school.

Yet one incident remained unexplained that might have been a forerunner of others to come.

I had never heard then of what is called astral flight, the theory of the departure of the soul from the physical body at certain times, temporarily—particularly during sleep. At such times, although linked by a psychic cord, the psyche according to this belief is free to wander at will and to return later to the sleeping body.

One morning my father called me to come into the store. Inside I observed a woman customer who stared at me with an angry expression. I wondered what I had done to upset her, since to the best of my knowledge I had never seen her before.

My father did know her. She was one of his long-time customers, a respectable, entirely normal and proper person. However, what she said to me hardly fitted that description:

"Young man, you are in my room every night. I see you at the foot of the bed after I turn down the lights. I don't want you to come there any more."

I told her I had never seen her until that instant, and that I had never been to her room, day or night.

She vehemently maintained that her story was true and pleaded with my father to order me to stay away. My father knew the woman as a perfectly rational being. But he also knew her accusation could not be true.

All I knew was that in my conscious life I never had seen her before or been to her room as she claimed. But having no valid explanation that seemed to fit the facts, I dismissed the episode from my thoughts. There were other, more urgent concerns.

Time—and the war—ran on.

Those of military age were registered for military service but were allowed to continue working at Vickers until circumstances required their induction into the British armed forces. Eventually my age group was called to the colors, and after training we were told that we were going to the front lines in France.

But we did not go to France and the battlefronts. Every time we were on the verge of leaving—something happened. In one case, as we waited along with military units of veterans in Dover, ready to board ship, a mutiny developed among some who did not want to return to the front. Instead of going into the trenches, our unit was held back to do special paper work. We issued railroad warrants and food-ration coupons to the soldiers of the mutineering units to distribute them to widely scattered parts of the country to forestall further disorders.

Later, when I was about to be sent abroad again, it was found that I needed glasses and I was sent not to France but to a hospital in London. The next time I was waiting to board the channel boat, our orders failed to come through. No one knew why. We waited—not hours but weeks. The orders had simply been lost. Twice more I was on the brink of departure and called back; one destination was the Dardanelles. In the last instance it was because the war was over.

I returned to Vickers to finish my apprenticeship. It was almost completed because under the law my time in the army counted in tabulating my indentured service. I also completed my courses at the Barrow Technical School. Of course I was still of very junior status in the company, just beyond the apprentice stage. I was now a journeyman. One day I received an order to report to the office of the chief engineer of the aeronautic section. The chief engineer himself wanted to see me. This was quite unusual.

He was a big man, very calm and sure of himself. He told me to sit down. He seemed to be looking me over. Apparently satisfied, he asked me what I would think of becoming an aeronautical engineer.

Here was the chief engineer of the company asking me to join his staff. I asked him, "Why do you pick me? What makes you certain I can do it?"

His answer was to lift up my education records and marks and my work records in the plant. "These tell me you could make a fine engineer."

With great pleasure and excitement I told him I accepted his offer.

At first they gave me only minor assignments, designing fittings and simple structures, which apparently I did to their satisfaction because I was favored with more and more complex problems as I gained experience and showed my ability.

Then came a contract for the R-80, a new type of lighter-than-air dirigible, the first to be designed with an envelope covering without parallel sections, actually in the shape of an elongated teardrop. The teardrop shape brought in complex structural design problems involving stresses in continuous beams. I was given responsibility for the longitudinal and transverse girders, the full-length walkways, one on top of the envelope and one underneath, the engine and flight controls, and the bow mooring gear. This airship was successfully flight tested.

The next project was a 100,000 pound seaplane, a great opportunity and challenge in those days. But the whole exciting plan blew up in a single slip of paper canceling the order. The project had been called off because of the sharp depression sweeping across England immediately after the war. The engineering force at Vickers was reduced by 80 per cent, and I was one of those laid off. The staffs of most of the industries in town were drastically reduced for the same economic reason. No business, or home, remained unaffected. Moving to avoid open rebellion and violence by millions without jobs, funds, or food, the government inaugurated a new national program almost as disastrous as depression: the dole. Stay at home—and collect your money at the end of each week. A whole nation was being turned into a charity list. No one was working. Many spent their time playing billiards or cards. Jobs were nonexistent. No Help Wanted signs were everywhere.

I, too, was unable to get a job. I took additional studies in night school, however. And I did attempt to find work, even going north to Manchester and other cities nearby, but without any luck. For a time I accompanied a traveling salesman who had a light automobile. We moved from town to town on the back roads of England. We made very little money stopping in at the farms along the way, sometimes driving up a path a mile or two to the farmhouse so that the farmer's wife could purchase a package of pins or needles, or perhaps a knot of tape.

I learned something about farm-to-farm selling and gained an enviable knowledge of the back roads of the English countryside. It was fun and healthy, but not monetarily rewarding.

During this same period of life, however, there came a revival of psychic experiences which had, for a number of years, been almost dormant.

One was a prophetic symbol—grim, chilling, frightening—that I would see over the head of a man or a woman, a small thin skeleton near which was a number. Always it was a digit between one and nine.

At first I had no idea at all what this meant, and having no idea or suspicion, I would blandly tell the individual what I saw. Within the time indicated by the digit, someone connected with that person died.

In each instance it was the same. If I saw a six—in six days, or six weeks, or six months the individual died. I learned from experience that the size of the number had a meaning: The larger digit meant days, the medium size meant weeks, and the small size meant months.

This happened on a number of occasions. I could no longer doubt what these skeletons implied: a precognition of death.

I did not want to see them. I tried to keep from any impression or impulse to speak of them. But the story spread and there were actually people, including close friends, who grew afraid to talk to me.

The psychic phenomena kept on for a period of several years. At last, one day, after another experience of this nature, I cried out angrily, "I hope I never see those skeletons again."

From that moment on, the skeleton phenomena ended. Soon after the skeletons ceased to appear, I was to have an experience even more shocking to me and my family.

My sister Edith, whom I loved with a deep affection, stayed in bed for a day with a seemingly minor ailment, described in the vernacular as being "out of sorts"; we believed it was not in any way serious. Edith was at that time teaching piano daily in a studio she had set up across the street from our house. She did quite well. She had seventy-five pupils.

Being "out of sorts" was nothing; she would rest a day in bed, that was all. After breakfast that morning, because of the damp weather we all drew up chairs around the fireplace. A feeling came over me. Without knowing what impelled me, I heard myself saying, "Edith is going to die."

My mother, horrified, told me to be quiet; I should not say things like that. I said, "Edith is going to die."

That was all.

I did not and do not know what drove me to say this. It was not merely that I had the impression that this was going to happen. *I had to verbalize this impression.* I was compelled beyond my control to speak these words.

The following morning, at four o'clock, my sister Edith died.

The doctor reported that she died from acute nephritic congestion. Yet love her as I did, I did not grieve as greatly as the others, for I seemed to know that she was not really dead, that she had passed on into another life that was equally real. I seemed to know this because I had known what was going to happen.

Not all the psychic events I experienced in that rather postwar era in England were so grim. One which occurred long before the death of Edith was, in fact, for me an important beginning in psychic therapy. My sister Barbara had suffered an injury to her neck, leaving her head twisted to one side in a virtually fixed position. She could move it only an inch or two, with great pain and difficulty. Doctors who examined her said that the injury was permanent and she would live her life out with this condition which, they stated, would grow more firmly established as cartilage grew around the injured area.

It did not occur to me that I could do anything to help. Healing of the sick had not become a part of my life at that time. One Saturday morning, however, I was in the sitting room of our home at 247 Rawlinson Street, Barrow-in-Furness, reading a newspaper. I remember that my interest was centered on a soccer game which was to be played that day. The newspaper had a sports editorial about one of the great players of our local team, a goalkeeper named Campbell. The editorial referred to Campbell as a "magnificent" player on whom the fate of the team depended. I was so engrossed in the sports stories and opinions about the game that I hardly noticed my sister Barbara, sitting in the same room, crocheting. Outside, it was a sunny, cool Saturday morning in early fall.

My first intimation that something was happening of an unusual nature came when the morning newspaper I was holding began to grow heavy in my hands. This was an experience of a nature unknown to me before—or since.

The newspaper became leaden-weighted in my hands. Strong as I was, I could hardly hold it. The heaviness seemed to increase second by second. My hands were forced down to my lap; the newspaper fell to the floor.

I wondered if the paralytic condition of my sister's neck had by some chance become contagious. I seemed to be helpless in the grip of this force.

A moment later another sensation came over me. I felt a mass emerging out of my solar plexus. This extrusion was perhaps eight inches in diameter and emerged from my body as much as ten inches. The sensation was so real that I looked down and was startled to see—nothing. The next instant I felt the force, the same force that seemed to drag the paper down, tugging at this psychic substance or mass, pulling me out of this chair, and across the room, drawing me to my sister's chair.

Here my hands, of their own volition, went out and touched the sides of Barbara's neck. This was my only actual physical contact with my sister. It lasted no longer than five or six seconds. But my sister's neck straightened. Her paralysis was suddenly—

and completely—gone. She was able to move her neck freely, without pain or difficulty.

Curiously, little was said by either of us during this unusual experience. It all happened too swiftly. I can remember only that Barbara said, "Look! I can move my neck."

All of this happened as if we were going through a kind of dream sequence in which logic becomes illogic and vice versa. None of it seemed real, but it obviously was. The proof was there; Barbara's neck was no longer twisted.

The whole thing seemed preposterous. I wanted an explanation for myself, not in psychic but in scientific terms that I could accept. My mind seized on one aspect of the nonmetaphysical world that had already become widely accepted and socially respectable: the subconscious mind. Could my subconscious somehow have obtained the information that if I went to her and touched a nerve point in her neck she would be well? But this was absurd. What mind transmitted this information? Besides, what had I done beyond touching lightly the sides of her neck? How could that cure her?

Barbara, with feministic intuition, accepted it on its face value. Something, somehow, had cured her neck after the doctor told her it couldn't be corrected and she would be like that all her life. She was happy about it, but did not understand it. Nor did I.

In this era of doles, closed factories, and no jobs, many youths were turning to sports and recreation. There was so little else to do. I continued with my studies, taking courses in various subjects and higher mathematics. I read a great deal.

But I still had time, and one day, upon the invitation of some friends, I dropped in at the local YMCA to register. After registering, I was standing in the lounge with a number of young men gathered around a potbellied stove. There was considerable discussion going on and no one paid much attention to me. I stood there in silence.

A man came out of a tiny office in the back. His name, I was to learn, was John E. Cockerill, secretary of this YMCA branch, and a Methodist Lay Preacher.

He crossed the room to the area where we all were standing and stood a moment, undecided. He looked at me for a long moment. Then he asked me to come with him into his office.

I thought he was about to give me a lecture on my duties and obligations as a new member of the "Y." Instead, when we reached his office, he merely told me to sit down in a chair alongside a conference table; he sat down in his desk chair, took something out of a drawer, and handed it to me.

The article was a bracelet of metal plates linked together with wire links. After handing this to me, he began writing a letter, as if he had forgotten that I was even in the room. I had no idea what I was supposed to do with this bracelet, or if I was to do anything with it at all.

4 ᣝ A Pot of Tea

I sat there for some moments, in this silence, idly examining the brass bracelet. I noticed some Greek letters and a human form engraved on the metal plates. I held the bracelet up to see the inscriptions in the light. As I did this, I felt a sharp deep-cutting pain across my back, like the lash of a long leather whip.

Startled, I turned in the chair to see what or who was behind me. There was nothing and no one.

Mr. Cockerill looked up from his letter writing with a mildly interested expression. "What's the matter?"

"I don't know," I said. "I thought someone hit me with a whip."

He had a little smile on his lips. He said, "All right. You can give me back that article now."

My answer to that was to ask him sharply, "What is this?"

"It's a bracelet."

"I know it's a bracelet," I said. "What hit me?"

He said, "Oh—you felt someone strike you with a whip."

"How? There's no one behind me, you're writing a letter at your desk. No one else in the room. How could anyone hit me with a whip?"

"All right," he said, relaxing somewhat. "I honestly don't know if I can explain it to you so that you can understand it. You see, I was sitting here, writing this letter, when I was suddenly aware that there was a sensitive outside."

"What do you mean by that?"

"A sensitive," he explained, "is someone subject to psychic or spiritual influences. When I received this impression I got up from my letter, walked outside into the main room, and looked over the people who were there." He paused. "You were the only one I didn't know. It had to be you."

"Why? Am I different from the rest of those fellows?"

I was neither annoyed nor angry; I was curious. Once again, these forces I did not understand were pressing close to me.

"Yes, you are different," he said. "I'm afraid you really are. Anyway, I decided to test you. You have demonstrated that you are indeed a sensitive."

I said, "That lashing across my back? Who knows what it means? That could be anything or nothing."

"It *could*. But it isn't just anything—or nothing. I gave you the bracelet, knowing that if I left you alone you would examine it. I wanted to see if you could feel anything about it."

There is a field of psychic investigation known as psychometry, built on a metaphysical concept that impulses come to the sensitive in psychic emanations from some article the sensitive holds.

"The bracelet," he informed me, "was worn by a girl who was a slave in northern Africa. It was taken from her body, according to its documented history, after she was whipped to death."

"How could I feel a whiplash or anything else out of that bracelet?" I demanded.

"The theory," he said, "is that the plates are impregnated with this violent event. And because of your psychometric gift you were able to receive this metaphysical imprint of its history, like a record that is played back."

I had never heard or read anything about this theory. To me the explanation sounded, to use the mildest term, farfetched. The fact that a girl would be beaten to death with a whip was possible, but unlikely. I decided that I had been hypnotized.

With the frankness of youth and my basic need for answers I could accept, I told Mr. Cockerill that I was convinced he had hypnotized me.

He did not seem unduly provoked by my brash assault on his integrity. Instead, he merely asked me how he could have hypnotized me while writing a letter and not saying a word or even glancing up in my direction.

I told him I simply didn't know. Possibly, it wasn't hypotism. But I still did not and would not accept his explanation.

He then asked me if I would be willing to try another experiment to test my sensitivity. While I had no great desire to do so, I was still curious enough to agree. I asked him what he wanted me to do. All he said was "Sit quietly. Don't try to do anything. And if you see—or feel—anything, inform me at once."

There could be no danger or harm in this, I decided. Besides, there was a door close by through which I could dive into the hall outside if I had to. I sat back in the chair and tried to relax. I closed my eyes. As I did so, I saw a man very clearly. It was not just a mental image; this was truly an impression of almost tangible plasticity. I could even see that the man was wearing a red vest.

When I told Mr. Cockerill what I was seeing, he asked me to describe the man's face. I did so with as much detail as I could. Mr. Cockerill then arose, left the room, and came back in about three minutes, carrying a black-and-white photograph. Was this, he wanted to know, a photograph of the man I had seen in my mind?

I told him I was absolutely certain that it was.

"Do you know who it is?"

"No."

"His name is William Thomas Stead," Mr. Cockerill said. "He died in the sinking of the *Titanic*."

I asked him what the picture had to do with him or the YMCA. He then related the following unusual history:

Mr. Cockerill never knew William T. Stead in life. Stead lived in London and had a reputation as an editor. Soon after the *Titanic* went down, Mr. Cockerill, while working alone in his office, would feel a lapping of waves around his feet, rising gradually like water and covering his entire legs and body. He began also to be aware of the presence of a man with him during these episodes. This, he became convinced, was William T. Stead. Stead did not speak and yet Mr. Cockerill knew psychically who he was.

Mr. Cockerill became so deeply engrossed in this experience that he went out and acquired a photograph of Stead from a dealer who collected such pictures and biographical material about personalities.

Mr. Cockerill then pointed out that I had known none of these facts. "Yet you came in here, sat down, and described in great detail a picture you could not have seen because I had it stacked away in another part of the building. Moreover, even if you had seen it, how could you have known that this face had meaning to me?"

I told him there could be a very simple explanation. "For some reason you wanted to impress me," I said. "So you sat there and thought of Mr. Stead's picture, holding it in your mind, and I got it through thought transference. It's as easy as that. You projected the image."

"But I wasn't even thinking about Mr. Stead," he protested. "Besides, the only picture I ever saw of him is this one here—a black and white. How could I project the red vest you described?"

"Did he wear a red vest that you know of?" I asked.

"I have no idea."

"Perhaps that detail I gave was incorrect. Or perhaps you saw a colored picture of him in some magazine. He was a prominent man; his picture has been in magazines."

He insisted that he had never seen such a picture.

"Perhaps you did without realizing, and it remains in your subconscious."

I was not being difficult simply to make myself unpleasant. Nor did I dislike Mr. Cockerill as an individual. I knew nothing about him beyond what had happened. But I was determined, at all costs, to accept nothing on face value, certainly none of that afternoon's episodes.

Mr. Cockerill, following our experiment, wrote to the daughter of Mr. Stead and asked about the vest. The daughter replied, in a letter I later saw, that her father had owned a red vest and on occasion delighted to wear it.

But on that first day I was sure Mr. Cockerill was putting these things into my mind. I said I did not know how I did this, but I could see no other rational explanation. He said all right, he would try another test. "Let's see if, by projection alone, I can put an idea into your mind."

He took out a watch which he set to various times arbitrarily, then asked me to try to "see" the time to which the watch hands pointed. In every instance, without exception, my guess was incorrect. "If I can project facts into your mind," he said, "why can't I project these various times to which the watch is set?"

I didn't accept that as any proof at all. He could be looking at the watch but actually thinking about a time different from that indicated on the watch.

I was accepting nothing that day. In fact, I really thought this nice-appearing, pleasant-talking secretary of the local YMCA was a little touched in the head. He suggested we would talk about other tests later. I agreed. I went out into the lounge and joined the others there. They were all talking about soccer, which seemed far more normal and interesting and at least I understood the subject. The psychic world was a poor competition when opposed by a soccer match.

But I did become a frequent participant in sports and other activities at the YMCA, and I became quite friendly with Mr. Cockerill, who interested me in many of the activities, including chess and billiards. He did not bring up psychic matters directly nor did we try any more experiments.

Nevertheless, there were indications that lines of force were directing me toward the psychic, toward areas quite different from any charted by my own inclinations.

Some weeks later there were to be a series of lectures—travelogs —in a local theater for the general benefit of the YMCA, under the overall direction of Mr. Cockerill. One afternoon while I was at the "Y," he came to me in obvious agitation. "A bundle of tickets to the lectures is missing. They represented a good many pounds in value."

These were tickets the "Y" would sell to residents of the community. If they were not found, Mr. Cockerill said, the "Y" would lose a considerable sum of badly needed funds. He didn't believe any member of the "Y" would have taken them, but there were many drifters in the neighborhood who might have wandered in and picked up the tickets if they were left unattended. I was standing at that moment beside a long wooden cabinet used at parties as a serving board, and inside of which was storage space for books and records. As I looked down at the wooden top, I found myself looking through the wood itself, directly into a drawer below. In that drawer I saw quite distinctly the misplaced tickets.

"No one took them, Mr. Cockerill," I said. "They are there in the drawer. There is a drawer in this counter. I can see it."

"Of course," he said. "It's used by the secretary of the Badminton Club. He keeps supplies and records there. But why would he have these tickets?"

"Well, I can see them," I said.

The drawer proved to be locked. Mr. Cockerill thereupon sent for the secretary of the Badminton Club, a reliable and quite substantial member of the community.

The secretary said, "I don't know why you called me but I'm glad you did. This morning I saw a pile of tickets left on the top of this counter. You know how the drifters come into this place in the morning, looking for handouts. I didn't think leaving the tickets out there on the counter with nobody around was a good idea, so I put them away for safekeeping."

He opened the drawer. The pile of tickets lay there exactly as I had seen and described them to Mr. Cockerill.

Mr. Cockerill, who was himself a clairvoyant and had many years of experience with this extrasensory gift, was not in the least surprised. He accepted this involuntary demonstration of my "gift" as something quite normal in view of our earlier experiments.

Another important milestone on this road occurred a few weeks later. Mr. Cockerill was to give a lecture at the "Y" in the large concert hall which paralleled the lounge. We had become quite friendly. He asked me if I were going to attend the lecture and, if so, would I be willing to help him clear away the chairs afterward. I told him I would be glad to. After the lecture we started moving the chairs to the sides of the big room. Mr. Cockerill was at one end of the room and I at the other, perhaps fifty feet apart, when suddenly I saw over his head what looked to me at first like a ball of light. As I watched there appeared in the center of this cloudlike effect—a teapot. I called to Mr. Cockerill, "I see something above your head."

Again, quite matter-of-factly, he inquired, "What is it you're seeing?"

"I see a kind of cloud and in the middle—a china teapot."

"Describe the teapot," he ordered.

I described the design, colors, complex pattern. It was a colorful decorative design.

"What you are describing," he said, "is one of my wife's most prized possessions."

At that instant I saw this teapot in the cloud above his head smashed into bits before my eyes. I told him what I was seeing. He said that this could not possibly be correct. "The teapot is very precious to us. My wife guards it very carefully. It is on a top shelf in our china cupboard at home and no one touches it or goes near it in our house. So you have to be wrong in this regard."

This was on a Saturday night. (We were in fact clearing the place of chairs so that it could be used for other purposes on Monday morning.) We left the hall that night about ten o'clock. The following morning I dropped over to the "Y." The first person I ran into was Mr. Cockerill, and the first thing he said was "Ambrose, I broke the teapot. Right here, this morning."

"How could you do that? I thought you said it was on the top shelf in your cupboard."

That, he said, was what he had thought. But a group of ladies of the Badminton Club of the YMCA had dropped in late, while a lecture was in progress, and, unknown to Mr. Cockerill, his wife loaned them the teapot with their promise to be extremely careful in handling it.

After the party was over, they left the teapot on a long sideboard used for such functions, a sideboard over which there were three shelves, about thirty feet long, on which were kept biscuits, candy, soft drinks, and similar items. Mr. Cockerill had arisen early the following day, on Sunday, to do some work in his office; he grew thirsty as he worked and decided to go in and get a soft drink. As he reached for a bottle of his favorite mineral water, he knocked down another bottle which plunged off the shelf—down upon the teapot which he had not noticed until he saw it lying before him, smashed, precisely as I had seen it in the cloud above his head the previous evening.

Mr. Cockerill could not have been fabricating this story. Too many people knew the circumstances—the ladies of the Badminton Club, his own wife, and other members of the "Y." Moreover, I had learned to know him and to realize that he was an honorable and honest individual. Further, he was not about to smash up deliberately one of his wife's highly valued pieces of crockery merely because I had seen it being smashed in a cloud the previous night!

To look into the future one had to take into account the key factor of time. Many things cannot even be thought of without the element of time. Time is intimately related to space; if you remove the one you cannot have the other. Yet I had apparently moved ahead in time. I could not explain that by any physical laws that I knew. Coincidence seemed out of the question; it was too detailed an experience, the vision and the ensuing reality were too exactly congruent; it could not have been mere chance.

Could it have been Mr. Cockerill's subconscious mind? Could he have *subconsciously* seen the teapot that he thought was at home and, reacting subconsciously, deliberately knocked over the bottle that fell on it, to make my prediction stand up? That seemed even more preposterous. And what of the high improbability of his hitting the teapot with the bottle in such a subconscious maneuver from the third shelf up? The odds again would be fantastic.

I could reach no satisfactory answer. But I was growing more and more aware of a personal need to explore the laws that were invoked in these phenomena I personally was experiencing. I was sure that there had to be here, as elsewhere in our lives, applicable and discoverable laws.

I felt I had to explore, to probe, to seek, to understand.

I joined a local psychic circle of perhaps six or seven persons who met regularly once a week. One woman who came regularly was a trance medium.

We would sit in semidarkness and messages would come. I would strive hard, at these scenes, to see or hear or feel something happening within me, but nothing happened. (It was only later that I began to understand that striving to contact psychic forces consciously was like throwing up a brick wall to ward off such experiences.) No messages came for me! There was, however, one very charming young lady who attended this circle, and I must admit that I continued to attend this circle, not so much to develop my relationship with the psychic world as to build my friendship with her.

One night, however, during a hush that had come over the room, I heard myself saying the following words: "The next time I go up a ladder, I will fall down."

As soon as I said this, I thought what a foolish thing for me to say—particularly since I never went up ladders. However, the words proved to be strongly prophetic. About a month later Lady Cavendish was paying a visit to our YMCA. Mr. Cockerill discussed with me the problem of how to decorate the concert hall where the reception would be held. The hall was in a dreadful state of disrepair; plaster was falling off the high walls in a number of places.

I told him I had a solution. In the drill hall of the nearby armory there were flags stored away which I was sure they would be happy to lend us for this important reception. "We'll all decorate the hall with the flags. They'll be colorful and will also cover up those bad patches."

We collected a large group of members to pitch in on this job. It was really a gala event, that flag-hanging party. In the midst of it I saw Mr. Cockerill looking up to the eaves. He pointed high up to where a spike was protruding out of the wall. "This hall used to belong to the Loyal Order of Moose," he told me. "They had a moose head up there. When they sold the hall, they took the moose head with them but left the spike."

"Why don't we drape a flag over the spike?"

It was a good idea, but how did we get the flag up there? I said all we needed was a very tall ladder. There had to be one in the school across the street.

There was. Mr. Cockerill and one of the boys went over and got it—a thirty-foot ladder. I put it up against the wall and saw that it did not quite reach high enough. But by stretching I could just slip the flag over the spike. The floor of the hall was highly polished. It was used for dancing, among other things. I asked another member who was working with the group to "hang on so it won't slip."

With him hanging on, I went up the ladder, almost to the highest rung, carrying the flag. I managed to get it over the spike, but the folds were not properly draped. I was trying to adjust them. Below me, the lad holding the ladder was called away to do some other job. The ladder began to slide along the highly polished floor; the top, with me clinging to it, began to slide down the wall. The ladder hit a row of coat hooks on the wall on which had been placed temporarily some steel uprights used with horizontal bars in the gymnasium. The ladder stopped when it hit these bars, but I kept on, plunging through the ladder, splitting the sides and knocking out several rungs, hitting a wooden table with my left leg and breaking the table.

I smashed face-first against the table, breaking my nose. I disentangled myself and stood up. The room was spinning. I saw a chair nearby and sat down. Soon there were forty or fifty people around me. Dazed, I heard someone say, "Look at the floor— there's blood all over the floor." With a big dish under me to catch the blood, I was carried to Mr. Cockerill's house. I could actually see the shinbone and a pulsating vein in my leg. But no bones were broken, although the gash was about six inches long and laid wide open. (I still bear the scar.)

A doctor was called. He got the bleeding stopped and stitched up the wound but did nothing for my nose. It was while he was taking care of me that I realized the words I had uttered in the darkness of the psychic circle: *The next time I go up a ladder, I will fall down.*

Two of the men from the "Y" group helped me get home that night. When I came in and started up the stairs, making one step at a time with great difficulty, my father called out to ask me what was the matter. I told him it was nothing. "I just bumped my leg a bit."

The doctor had told me to stay off my feet for two weeks.

But I had a date with a girl the following night and I wasn't about to let that accident keep me home. In Barrow-in-Furness on a date all you did was walk—five miles out and five miles back. So the next night I walked ten miles on that bad leg. It didn't bother me very much; I was too interested in the girl.

Many times I have thought about that sequence of events. How could I have known that the boy would walk away from the ladder? Or that the moment he did, it would fall? I had nothing to do with those things; I was on the ladder and the youth was thirty feet below. There was no way that I could have had an influence, consciously certainly, on this event. I doubt if anyone could accept the theory that I subconsciously compelled him to walk away from the ladder, even if I had wanted him to do this, and that could hardly seem possible in any case.

I have come to believe that we do not understand time, physically or metaphysically. I think it is an area that deserves the closest study by scientists employing the latest concepts, particularly with regard to sensitives and their predictions. I think we may find that the ability of certain individuals to "see" the future is something like moving time forward, as if we are seeing something that has already been generated in the unseen realm but not in the realm of the everyday existence around us. These events may then be simply waiting, like a train on a siding, for conditions to come about that will make the event possible in our so-called "real world."

In these early days in England these probings of the future seemed to come of their bidding, not mine, at moments when I was most relaxed and putting forth no effort whatever to contact entities or forces beyond ourselves.

Many things that happened seemed to follow no logical pattern or sequence whatsoever. I recall one instance at breakfast. I looked across the breakfast table at my sister Barbara's plate and saw a Canadian stamp on the plate. I knew it was not an actual stamp on her plate, not a stamp I could pick up. Yet it was "real" to me.

I told my sister, "You're going to get a letter from Amy in Canada."

Barbara scoffed at this as impossible. Amy had written Barbara three letters and had had no answer to any of them. "Amy isn't going to write me," she insisted.

But the morning mail contained a letter for Barbara from her friend Amy in Canada.

5 ❧ Space and Time

I could not discuss these events with many people. In a sense I was alone; although my parents and my sisters understood something of psychic things, most of what happened still left them puzzled, dubious, alarmed.

I had sought to dismiss these events, or to find explanations, but in most cases was not able to do so. Yet there was this record of events, a fact in my life with which I had to deal.

At an earlier date, when the woman who was one of my father's customers said she saw me at the foot of her bed each night after turning out the light, I could dismiss the whole thing as wild raving nonsense.

But at a later date—I believe it was in 1923—other events involving what is called astral projection took place that could not be easily dismissed; they happened directly to me, in my own experience. Further, conditions in the second instance were more controlled, the facts themselves more inexplicable.

This was a case in which I personally knew the entire story at first hand. I write out of personal knowledge. Either I am lying, or self-deluded to a point of rash idiocy—*or the episodes occurred as I describe them.*

I was at that time interested in a young lady. I will call her Marie. She and her sister, who played the organ in the church, were good friends of mine. I was especially attracted to Marie.

One night, after I had gone to bed, I found myself in the bedroom of Marie and her sister. *This was not a dream.* I was consciously aware of everything that was happening. I was not dreaming. It was as if I had left the sleeping self and been transported, by what means I do not know, into another room several miles away. I was there, hearing the two sisters talk. They were involved in some kind of heated discussion. I did not know and could not learn what it was about.

Moments later I awoke in my bed. But it was not the same as waking from ordinary sleep. I was conscious that I had been somewhere else and returned. I had a clear memory of the room and the sisters.

Several days after this I ran into Marie on the street and asked her, "What were you and your sister arguing about in your bedroom the other night?"

She looked a little startled and asked the night I spoke of.

"Wednesday last."

She said, "How in the world would you know about that argument?"

I said, "Oh, I was there."

"But you couldn't have been in our bedroom," she insisted.

"I was there," I said, "and that's how I know about it."

"You mean you were there in spirit?"

I said, "Well, I was there. I don't know how but I was. And I heard this discussion going on between you two. I don't know how I was there or how I got back to my body but I woke up and it was all very clear."

She said, "We were having a discussion that night. I wish you had done something, given some signal. If it ever happens again, try to give some sign to make us aware."

I told her I didn't expect that this would happen again but should it recur I would try to let them know.

About four weeks later I found myself undergoing the same experience in the bedroom of these sisters. The experience, so far as my own awareness was concerned, was as before. It was not a dream. I knew that my body lay back in our home on the bed. I knew that I was in the room looking at the two girls who were at that time asleep. I recalled clearly that Marie had urged me to give them a sign, to do something to show them that I was in the room with them.

I tried to speak to them but they did not rouse. I tried to touch them and shake them but I had no effect. So I bent down beside the bed and shouted at the top of my voice, "Marie, Marie, wake up!"

She opened her eyes and looked at me. She was looking directly into my eyes.

Immediately I awakened and found myself back in my bedroom.

The following morning Marie came down to the store. Obviously in a state of excitement, she said abruptly, "I saw you last night."

I said, "Where?"

"In our bedroom."

"What did I look like?"

She said, "I can't tell you because all I saw were your eyes. They were looking right into mine and then they disappeared."

This agreed exactly with what I recalled as having taken place.

The episodes piled up. They became harder and harder for me to deny, to reason away. They were thrust upon me and, frustrated in my desire to find reasonable explanations, I doubled my efforts to understand these forces by investigating the subject matter more fully.

Marie invited me to her home to witness a series of seances conducted by a trance medium. It was true that I still tried too hard to get "results" in these seances. I found them dull. Messages that supposedly came "through" the medium in trance were usually of no import to the general group, rarely of any significant value even to the individual receiving the message. The long period of quiet in the darkness sometimes lulled me into a quiet that was itself almost trancelike. One night during such a period of quiet I found that I was looking at the back of my own head. As this fact dawned on me, I realized that I was standing behind myself and could see myself sitting before me in that semidarkness.

This was a moment of unexpected terror. Despite all that I had seen in psychic experiments, I was not prepared for this incredible sensation of being out of my body, of actually looking at myself. Fear was magnified by the additional feeling that I would not be able to get back. I appeared to have no power of movement.

What was most frightening, I suspect, was the intensely vivid reality. My awareness was actually increased; the solidity of the room was never more real. It could not be a dream. This I knew, I was frightened and trying to get back into my own body. Unlike a dream in which we only see or know part of the experience we dream, fragmentary parts at best, I knew everything that was happening around me. I knew that the lady in the chair beside me, as I came near the chair, was trying to help me, that I was now standing and that I was struggling to open my eyes. I put her thumbs on my eyebrows and let her stroke the eyebrows and blow on my forehead. I don't know why I did these things, but I do know that I was again in my body, that I was awake, and that the episode happened not in any dream state but precisely as described here.

I will not deny that this experience alarmed me. It did. This was a severe physical jolt. It impressed upon me very clearly also, in very realistic terms, the fact that I, Ambrose Worrall, had a second life, a spiritual life, a spiritual body, that this spiritual body had senses, it could hear and see and function.

While attending a meeting on psychology, I met and became very friendly with a man who knew a great deal about psychic matters and was psychic himself. He lived in a suburb of Barrow-in-Furness and was by trade a carpenter. He and I conducted a number of psychic experiments.

These began the first night I went to see him at his home. As I was passing through my father's store, on my way out I was impressed to take with me an ordinary piece of chalk. I had no idea that we would conduct any experiments requiring the use of chalk.

He lived in a comfortable, well-kept home with his wife and children. We discussed many things. We tried a few experiments with a popular form of spirit writing, employing what we called in England then a "planchette," a heart-shaped piece of plywood about eight inches long and six wide, supported on two swivel casters, with a hole in the center at the heart's point large enough to hold a pencil. I received several messages through this planchette writing, including one that reportedly came from my sister Edith!

I was not sure whether this was a valid word from my dead sister Edith or merely some form of thought transference functioning through the planchette in automatic writing. In any event I was not unduly impressed by the messages received by means of this planchette. Then, quite by impulse, acting in a way that I could not understand, I jumped up from my chair as if some force were compelling me, rushed into the dining room, removed the cloth covering the dining-room table, took out the piece of chalk I had brought with me, and began to write out the alphabet in chalk letters on the top of their shining, well-kept table.

All of this I did without asking permission of my host or hostess or offering any explanation. They watched me closely but did not try to stop me in any way.

When I finished writing the alphabet, I told my friend to get me a plain water glass. This he did. I placed it upside down on the table. The three of us put one finger each on this upside down tumbler. It began to move and again, like the planchette, spelled out messages that appeared to have meaning, and answered questions correctly.

One of the sons, an engineering student, came into the room and, after observing for a time, declared, "Dad's pushing it."

I said, "Well, all right, let's blindfold him and see. If he is pushing, he won't be able to see the letters."

We blindfolded him. But the tumbler continued to answer questions correctly. The son then said, "Blindfold mother." We did this also. The glass continued to answer correctly what we asked.

At the son's further suggestion I took a newspaper and held it in front of me. We all three had our fingers on the tumbler as before. It continued to spell words correctly and answer questions. The son suggested that perhaps I was reading the minds of the others. To make this impossible, I read aloud from the paper while the glass spelled out the answers.

There was the test situation: two persons blindfolded; a third with his view blocked by a newspaper, reading aloud from the paper.

And the tumbler, with our fingers on it, continued to spell words, give messages, and answer questions. The son, after the manner of the typical engineer, was still skeptical of the source of the communications but was at a loss to explain the correct spelling of the words under the test conditions. He expressed his doubts as to the possibility that the communications were from souls who had departed this life. Then a strange thing happened. The spelling which had been faultless to this point suddenly seemed to be meaningless. Upon being informed that the messages were no longer intelligible, the blindfolds were removed from my friend and his wife's eyes, I put aside the newspaper and, following the movements of the glass, we had to agree that as far as we could understand, the sequence of letters touched conveyed no message. It was observed, however, that the pattern of letters was being repeated. They were written down and checked and this was found to be the case. A younger son came into the room to see what was going on, and he looked at the letters that were written on the pad and exclaimed, "Why, that is Welsh; my grandmother taught me that one sentence in Welsh when I visited her several years ago."

The grandmother had passed away soon after the boy's last visit with her. It is significant that the sentence spelled out in Welsh was the only sentence known by the grandson—and those participating in the experiment were unfamiliar with the Welsh language.

Were these experiments valid? My answer to that is they had to have some validity or these people, as well as I, had to be subconsciously or deliberately perpetrating a deception. But a deception on whom and for what? If any one of us were playing games of some sort, what would they possibly have to gain? We had no way of gaining anything, no advantage, profit, or benefit of any kind.

Moreover, both of the sons indicated little belief in any of these goings-on.

Nevertheless, one of the sons was to be involved—without his knowledge, I must add—in a far more fantastic experiment.

This came in a further experiment in the realm of astral projection. It actually occurred quite a few months later, after I left England and came to America. Before I left, my psychic friend and I agreed to attempt astral flights on a transatlantic basis.

I had never before engaged in such an undertaking on such a scale, but after I reached America, I did make several attempts in personal transatlantic teleportation. I made these efforts always at night, always after I had retired, always in the darkness.

In at least one instance I was sure that I had made it. The difficulties were immense, yet I felt I was there; there were shadows, darkness, buildings, but I was there, across the water, in the house. While there, I was very much impressed with one notion, that for reasons I did not know, I had to get a one-pound note to the younger son, a youth still in his early teens.

So convinced was I that the impression received was correct and actual that I mailed a letter to the boy with one pound enclosed in the form of a postal order.

I received a letter in turn from the father. He said his son had been planning to go to London with some friends, but the family lived on a limited budget and there was no extra "bulge" for such excursions. My note arrived just in time; the boy had proudly announced to his father, "Dad, I can go on that excursion to London."

Neither he nor his father realized the full implications because I had not yet written to the father explaining what had led me to send the money. The father, on his part, had been making efforts to reach me in the city to which I had gone—Cleveland, Ohio. I had had no word from him as to his results. But I did take note of one incident that seemed to me rather unusual: An alarm clock of mine had stopped in the early morning, exactly at two o'clock. The fact that the hands were exactly on the hour caught my attention.

A week later I received a letter from my psychic friend in England in which he said that he had finally made it to where I lived. He described the room in which I was staying with many precise details. It would have been hard to understand how he could have known or guessed so many details. And he concluded with the statement that he, while in my room, had stopped the hands of my run-down alarm clock at two o'clock.

There are compulsions we do not understand.

I was, I am convinced, driven by these forces in the direction of psychic healing.

Yet healing itself had no part in this at first. The single episode of my sister's neck did not mean that I had any sustained ability in healing, and beyond that I had, in adolescent years, little evidence of the healing touch.

Many individuals in the groups with whom I met, however, had heard of my psychic experiences, and some of them began to ask me if I could give them what they termed a "psychic treatment." Even my explanation that I had no gift in this area did not discourage them; I had some contact with the power, they insisted; would I not at least try to help them?

This is an appeal very difficult to turn from. After all, I was not doing them any harm; I was not telling them to leave their physicians; in fact, exactly the opposite: I insisted that they must see physicians and carry out medical orders. They urged nonetheless that I try to help them. I had no real choice. I told them I would try.

How? All I knew was to wait upon the impression. I had studied no book on spiritual healing. When someone asked me to help I could only respond by reaching a sense of calm. The cases were of many types, from broken limbs to arthritic conditions and serious tumors and cases of paralysis. How could I know if I could help any of them?

I would wait. An impulse would come to make "passes" with my hands. I did not know why. But the impulse was too strong to ignore and I would heed it, raising my hands, moving them lightly over an arm, a shoulder. Sometimes my hand would stop at a certain point and the man or woman would say, "Yes, that is it. That is where the pain is."

I would say a silent prayer. I would hold my hand a moment or two at this point of pain or trouble of some kind. Then, once more entirely by intuition or inspiration, I would know that I had done as much as I could.

Sometimes I would put my hand on a chest, or on the back of a neck, or on a knee or an ankle. It was entirely intuition; this was one development that I began to learn, to allow the impulse to direct me in what I had to do. I would tell the patients frankly that this was what I did and nothing more—this was all I could do.

Psychic techniques, like their physical counterparts, must be developed. Jesus over and over in the Gospels gives us examples of these techniques. Dr. Leslie D. Weatherhead in his famous book, *Psychology, Religion and Healing,* describes the many techniques employed by Jesus in healing. He points out that Jesus used whatever was needed. Describing the case of the deaf stammerer, as recorded in the Gospel of St. Mark, Weatherhead writes, "This interview took place in private. . . . Jesus took the patient out of the reach of the contra-suggestion of scoffers. Touching the ears and the use of spittle would strongly increase suggestion. Note Jesus looking up to heaven, which the deaf man would interpret as prayer to God. The man's feeling of isolation is ended. . . . Notice how Christ gives the man confidence and increases expectation. Saliva is used again. Fingers are put into the patient's ears and his tongue is touched. . . ."

There are instances in the healings in which Jesus is very plainly instructing his followers. In the case of Jairus' daughter who they say is dead, Jesus tells the father bluntly that she is not dead. The mourners are already weeping in the house; Jesus takes with him Peter, James, and John, disciples on whose faith, as Weatherhead points out, Jesus can rely. But also—disciples whom He guides and instructs. Here He gives an excellent example of methodology. He pushes out all the weepers and mourners; doubt and disbelief and negation have no place in healing. He explains to the three friends he has brought with him that the girl is not dead, but only asleep. And then, using a term of endearment, "My little gazelle," he tells her to waken.

And when she does, Jesus makes no great emotional scene. As Weatherhead points out in his analysis, "He then hands her to her mother with the simple words, 'Give her something to eat,' thus bringing matters down to humdrum, simple doing, so valuable to the nerves of both mother and patient, and keeping the latter from the curious eyes of the crowd outside."

From the time when I asked my Sunday School teacher about the blind man I passed on my way to Sunday School, I had maintained my interest in the healings of Biblical times and the ongoing insistence that there was no reason such healings could no longer be achieved.

The greater part of the recorded works of Jesus were in the field of healing, of spiritual therapy. And He indeed did instruct His followers to go forth and heal.

And so, in England, I began to respond to such requests with what little I knew, calling on and waiting for the inspiration that would tell me what to do.

To my astonishment, people began to report to me that they were getting better, or were actually healed, and very often they had real evidence to show me, including some interesting medical reports. This gave me encouragement to go on with these experiments. But I had no idea of their significance. And I did not, at that time, bother with such things as records.

But as the stories unfolded, word spread that I was a healer.

6 ❧ Voyage

Healer or not, psychic or not, I had my ambitions and plans for a life and future of my own apart from these other forces that took hold of me. And in England all doors at that time seemed to lead to nowhere. Conditions economically had grown only worse; the dole had dug only deeper into the national soul; factories were idle and rotting. Ahead lay only bleak roads as far as I could see.

I was working at the only job I could get: behind the counter in my father's stationery store. It was hardly the bright engineering career for which I had all these years prepared.

One day in June, 1922, a young man came into the shop whom I had not seen before. He had an American accent. I asked him what part of the country he came from. "Goose Creek, Texas," he said. "Finest city—for its size—in the whole world."

I asked him how a person would set about going to America.

"It's a free country," he said. "All you have to do is buy yourself a ticket and come on over."

After he left I began to think. I thought a long time that day and in days to come.

The more I thought, the more certain I became that my future lay in a land big enough for continuing opportunities. A land that still had open doors. And open factories.

But getting to America was not so easy as my friend from Goose Creek had indicated. For one thing I needed money. This required scrounging. My family gave me some; the rest I borrowed. I also had to have sponsors in America if I were going to stay permanently. This was not too difficult; so many people were leaving England for America that sponsoring groups and families were to be found in almost every major American community.

The sponsors whom I obtained resided—I like to think by the hand of smiling fortune—in Cleveland.

There were all the usual bustlings of preparations, admonitions, and worries, and at last I set off—with two hundred and fifteen other people headed for a new life in America. I had funds enough to carry me for a time. I had no job and no prospect of one. I knew no one in America personally.

But my ship pulled out of harbor into the open sea. The time had come, I said to myself. The tide for me had begun to run.

We landed in Boston because it was easier and quicker going through customs there. I had no difficulties getting through immigration. At the foot of the gangway an American official halted me with the question, "And where do you think you're going, young man?"

"To Cleveland, Ohio," I told him.

He thought a moment and asked, "Why?"

I said, "Maybe I'll meet a girl and get married there."

He grinned. "Okay, fellow, go on with you. I hope you find just what you want—here in America."

The gift of second sight is not always applicable to worldly matters. Travel, for example, finding your way around strange cities. I had quite an earthbound time getting from the pier in Boston to South Station. Then I almost boarded the wrong train and had further difficulties until finally, with the help of a kindly stationmaster, I located the right train and the right track.

When we neared Cleveland I didn't know which stop I was supposed to get off at. My sponsors had sent word that they would meet me at the station. A man sitting beside me in the train gave me directions. They proved to be totally wrong, with the result that I got off on the opposite side of the city from where I should have been. Then I boarded the wrong streetcar and had gone perhaps half an hour in the wrong direction before I discovered that error. At last, however, I reached the residence where I was to stay. Most of the people there were recent arrivals like myself. They seemed relieved at my arrival but slightly restrained in their joyous welcome. A small delegation had waited in vain over an hour for me at the Union Station in Cleveland.

They were fine people and I was happily settled. But I had no time to squander either in getting lost or in trying to see the sights. It was exciting for me to be here. In my heart almost from the first day I felt I was an American. I wanted to belong.

The following morning I set out to find myself a job.

To my astonishment conditions in the United States, at least in Cleveland, were not too sharply different from what I had seen in the tight little isle of England. *Help Wanted* advertisements were limited, calling for specific qualifications and experience I didn't have. Most of the plants I visited either had *No Help Wanted* signs out or were taking only a few men—with hundreds waiting in line.

I walked a long way that day. I applied at nearly a dozen major companies. By late afternoon, weary, dusty, and disappointed, I found myself in the outskirts of the city at the main plant of the Glenn L. Martin Aircraft Company. There were perhaps seventy-five men waiting to be interviewed. It was a rather hopeless picture. I was last in line, I was a foreigner, and I had a broad English accent. I debated whether to stay or go on and try one more place somewhere else. Literally worn out from walking, I decided to wait. There were benches. I could sit down.

The moments ticked away. While I sat on a bench, the rows of waiting men ahead of me grew thinner. I was the last person left in the interviewing room.

A man came out of an inner office. He saw me and asked, "Are you waiting for someone?"

I managed a smile. The question seemed to sum up the whole

day. "No, I'm not really waiting. I have no appointment. And apparently, from the looks on everybody's face as they left, there are no jobs. So why should I take up your time? You must have other things to do."

He said in a kindly way, "Not at all. Come on in. Sit down. We can have a talk."

I went inside with this man and we talked. We talked about mechanical things, about aircraft and aircraft engines, and other topics with which I was familiar because of my work at Vickers, Ltd., years of apprenticeship before that, months of special studies after I left Vickers. I showed him my indenture papers and my marks in student years.

He seemed impressed. He asked a lot of questions. He asserted that there were no jobs open, that people were being turned away. "But we can always make room for an exceptional worker," he added, "if you don't mind low pay." I assured him I didn't.

We talked some more. It was already dark outside. He kept probing my knowledge of various areas involved in airplane production. Most of the answers I knew.

"Wait here," he said finally.

He got up and walked outside into the shop. When he came back, he was grinning. "You are about to take an important step," he told me. "You're going to work as a shop helper for the Glenn L. Martin Aircraft Company. This is the United States. I don't want to hear about how they do it in England. You start tomorrow."

I was there the following morning—at seven.

Again, with no psychic intuition whatsoever, I did not realize that I was about to be given a rather rugged introduction to the methods by which things are done in America.

The work actually began at 7:15 A.M.

I was taken to the foreman. He reached over, picked up a pair of pulley brackets, put them into my hand and said, "Put these on."

Then he got up and left. For a moment I was startled. Then I thought, "Well, maybe this is the way they do things in America." The last place I had worked for was Vickers, in the aircraft engineering department. I recognized that these pulleys were used to run cables through wiring and rigging of the aircraft. I went out into the shop and looked around. I saw some plans tacked up on a board, and I went over and studied them. On the plans were indications of places where pulley brackets like these appeared to be called for.

Nearby I saw some aircraft spars. The plans I had examined indicated that the brackets were for these spars. On several spars they had already been attached. On others they hadn't. I reasoned that my boss intended me to put these pulley brackets on those that had none. I stood a moment, wondering where I could get tools, when a man came up and asked if he could help me. I said, "Yes, I have to get an electric drill and some reamers so that I can put these pulley brackets on." He took me down to the tool crib, and I got the proper tools with which to work. This was before the days of expensive drill jigs. Most jobs like this one required skilled and exacting work by hand, with the holes laid out by hand measure, and the holes had to be drilled and reamed without the benefit of any drill jig bushings. However, I was quite a skilled mechanic and I laid out the holes, drilled them, reamed them, and bolted the pulley brackets in place, after which I went back to the foreman's desk and waited for him to return.

About nine o'clock he came back. A tall man, well over six feet, he made quite a figure. When he saw me a smile came over his face. "So you got stuck," he said, as if this were a familiar story.

"Not at all," I said. "I'm waiting for the next job. I finished that one."

He looked astonished. "And what did you do with the pulley brackets?" he demanded.

"I put them on."

"On *what?*"

I told him. He went over to the spar and he looked. Then he got the factory inspector and he told him that I was a new man, I had just assembled these pulleys. He would like them checked.

The inspector turned to me and said, "You are supposed to call me and let me check the size of the holes and the fit of the bolt before you put the pulleys on there. Now I don't know whether the holes are the right size or not."

I assured him that they were accurate, but he had to see for himself. So I undid the bolts and allowed him to check to be sure everything was in order, which it was. Then I replaced the bolts and the fitting.

Months later I learned from the foreman himself that no new man had ever done such a thing to him before. It was his custom with all new men to hand them the pulleys or some other component and go off for a couple of hours. Invariably on his return, they had done nothing.

So my "initiation" turned out to have an unexpected twist.

However, I had won his respect, and in the days that were to follow, he tested me in a number of ways.

The most significant of the early challenges came a few days later when he asked me to assemble an airplane propeller. He pointed out the blades, the fixtures, the hub, all the parts. He handed me the assembly drawing. All it showed was the angle of the blade at the forty-two-inch station from the hub. I looked at the angle on the drawing, and the fixture itself, some twenty feet away from me, and I told the foreman, "This fixture as it is now is no good."

He said, "I don't understand you."

I said, "The fixture has the blade at the wrong angle. It is not the angle of the drawing."

The foreman had the fixture returned to the tool department where the inspector checked it over and reported that it was perfectly in order. The foreman asked me to go with him to the inspector.

We went over the whole question with all of their implements. Then I saw what the error was. "You've measured correctly," I told him. "The trouble is you are using the sine of the angle, where you should be using the cosine."

Reluctantly, the toolmaker and the inspector had to confess this was correct. In the building of this assembly fixture both the toolmaker and the tool inspector had made the same error in interpreting the drawing. This error, if it had not been detected, could have resulted in the failure of the airplane to take off.

More and more difficult jobs were handed to me. I was given another job testing the riveted joints in the plane, testing for stress and strain on the body of the plane itself. It involved extremely complex mathematical computations. The care with which the company investigated every aspect of its products was nowhere better exhibited than here; we made literally thousands of tests. Many times my findings proved expensive, indicating the need for additional research, changes, and improvements. There were some at the plant who at first questioned whether this newly arrived Englishman Worrall knew whereof he spoke. But the tests bore out what I had said—as, for instance, in the case where a casting under test conditions broke—as I had known it would. Not because there were too few rivets but too many, and improperly spaced on the spar. They began to accept the fact that in aeronautic technical theory and practice I was reasonably sound.

I was proud of this beginning in America. I was making friends, going to parties, particularly in English-American circles in Cleveland. I continued with my religious and spiritual life; I was invited to join a small group of professional men and women making special investigations in psychic matters. I was attending night school classes in advanced technical fields.

The world into which I had walked was an exciting challenge. It was new, it was moving forward, it offered unlimited horizons, and I was part of all of this exuberant activity.

I did not have the least suspicion that psychic forces of the sort I had known all my life were, even then, apparently at work shaping what was to be the next important step in my life.

This involved a young lady whom at that time I didn't even know.

PART II ❧ MINISTRY

This part of our story, our healing ministry, is to us the most important and meaningful of our record. We are aware that much of what we write of psychic incidents may be difficult for many persons to understand or even accept; we do not try to impose ourselves or our beliefs upon others. It may well be that many can accept the facts as related and put upon them an interpretation totally different from our own.

In our opinion it is not correct to speak of our ministry as one of miraculous healing or faith healing. It is healing. It is normal, natural, a part of the law of God's universe. It is miraculous in the sense only that all of God's laws are miraculous. Whether the individual is aware of it or not, we all must live by these immutable laws. Not by bread alone, but by the bread of the spirit. Not by our laws alone, either, but by the laws of Spirit.

But in the application of these laws, we shape by our own actions. We must love people, we must want to help people. We must live by the laws, not of sickness but of health, by the laws not of hate, resentment, fear, but of love, forgiveness, expectancy. We must love our fellow man, we must want to minister to his need and his hunger, his pain.

7 ❧ Announcement

She was twenty-one years old. She had finished her education and was working as a private secretary in a business office in Cleveland. In addition she carried on an extremely active social life. Vivacious and pretty, she liked parties and laughter, music and dancing. At the same time she was active in the Russian Orthodox Church in which she had been brought up, and played her part in the smooth operations of the large house where she lived with her parents and her innumerable brothers and sisters. For Olga Nathalie Ripich, born November 30, 1906, the combination of work and family life and the rush of social activities provided an exuberant pattern of life in that December of 1927.

Yet it was in the very midst of that glittering pattern of activities that events began to occur which puzzled and disturbed her. And the rest of her family.

One night in the second week of that December, after she had retired to her bedroom and turned out the light, lying awake in the darkness, she began to hear knocking on the wall, in the dresser, and then in the cedar chest. The knocking started rather slowly and quietly. Gradually it grew louder and faster. Within a few minutes it had become so loud that it could be heard throughout the house.

The first night these noises were heard, the knocking lasted perhaps five to ten minutes—long enough to rouse the household. Olga's mother thought it must be Olga herself making the noise, and she came into the bedroom and demanded to know why

Olga was making all this racket. "You're waking everybody up," she stated.

"I'm not making these noises, mother," Olga said. "I don't know who or what is making them."

The noises continued.

A few seconds later the noises stopped abruptly. The family went back to sleep. The next night, however, they started again. This time Olga's mother, after examination, decided that it must be branches of the trees outside banging in the wind against the side of the house.

An investigation showed beyond any question that this theory was untenable. The branches were not close enough to bang against the wood side of the house even in strong December winds. The knocking continued the following night. And the next. It would go on for about ten minutes each night in Olga's room. The entire family heard it.

Mrs. Ripich finally told her daughter, "We've got to do something to stop this; it is driving us all insane. We are sleepless in the house. There is a woman from the old country who knows of these things. I am going to talk with her, Olga."

Olga, with all the impatience and self-assurance of youth, told her mother, "Mother, I don't believe in *old ladies from the old country*. It's all a lot of superstition."

"But the noises aren't superstition," her mother pointed out as she made the sign of the cross.

And the noises went on.

The woman Olga's mother intended to visit for help was one of those with a wealth of knowledge of old wives' tales. They know old spells and rituals and conjure up old sayings and beliefs to explain such things as these knockings in the night. (Although Olga had many psychic experiences in her youth, nothing like these rappings that came in the night, always after all the lights were extinguished, had ever occurred to her before.)

About a week after the noisy intrusions began Olga's mother went to the woman and told her the story. The woman at once decided that Olga was bewitched and that the spell had to be broken. There was a formula used for centuries in certain districts, she said. Olga was to spat on her petticoat three times, jump on her petticoat, and then wipe the petticoat over her face.

Olga's mother returned and told her what the old woman had said Olga must do. Olga refused. She said it was crazy and she wasn't bewitched and she refused to go through these rituals. That night, however, the knocking grew louder and more disturbing to the entire household. In the morning Olga's mother said, "You will do as I say—you will carry out those instructions as the woman directed. If there's no truth in it—all right. But it can't hurt. And I can't go through these sleepless nights with this disturbance."

To calm her mother, Olga reluctantly agreed to do this. She took off her petticoat, spat on it three times, trampled on it on the floor, and wiped her face with it—all as ordered.

"All right, now I've done it," she told her mother dutifully. And then added, "And we'll see if anything happens. Anyway, these noises seem friendly to me, as though they were trying to tell me that something wonderful is going to happen to me."

What occurred was that the noises and banging became worse that night than at any previous time. And Olga told her mother, "You see, it didn't work. That old woman and her spells! Whatever is causing this thing, I know this much—I'm not bewitched and I'm not afraid."

It was about a week later that my role in this began when a young man who happened to be president of a college club to which Olga belonged invited me to accompany him to a Christmas party that was to be given in a private home. Members of the club took turns giving parties in their homes, he explained. This Christmas party happened to be given in the home of Olga Ripich. So I went with this young man to Olga's Christmas party.

That was how we met. And from the very first moment I found

myself caught by Olga's fair-haired beauty. Something else happened also that startled me, although I did not speak of it to her at that time. I had the feeling, almost the certainty, that I had seen her or met her before, that we had known each other on a totally different level of existence.

It was as if we were not strangers.

I have already noted elsewhere that psychic gifts often do not work at all in the merely mundane matters of life. Apparently romance is in this category. In any case, neither Olga nor I had any extrasensory perception that the other party had interest in psychic matters of any sort.

Certain factors did work for us. At the party, for example, everyone gave and received a gift, chosen by chance. Mine was from Olga. And after I had left the party I discovered I had forgotten the gift on the piano. This gave Olga the opportunity to write a note, asking me to drop by and pick it up. Even before I received this letter, however, I had written one of my own—in verse, as it happened; I had discovered that Olga's original invitation was in verse.

All this note-writing, gift-giving and gift-leaving and picking up, served to bring us together. Within a few days we were going out on our first date. I think we both knew, almost from the first evening, what this meant, even if psychic intuitions were not functioning at high level. Perhaps it was normal and proper for us to find ourselves and our mutual interests in the self-discovery of all people falling in love.

Within two weeks I knew that I was in love with Olga. I was worried about this other aspect of my life—the psychic aspect—and how I should best explain it to her. I did begin to drop an occasional word or sentence to indicate some interest in that field; these were hints, testing words. I was somewhat surprised, in fact, that she seemed to understand so much of what I was trying to tell her. Neither of us, however, made any open commitment, each was afraid of driving away the other.

Within a very few weeks I knew that I wanted to marry Olga and I told her so. By that time I think we were both sure in our hearts. Long after we were married, Olga told me, "The night you asked me to marry you—I felt as if I had come home."

The Christmas party at which we met took place on December 27. I proposed to Olga on February 4.

Once she had accepted, I realized that I had to tell her fully and openly about the psychic side of my life. In as simple, realistic a way as I could, I told her of the various events that I had experienced.

At that moment, as I related these things, I felt I was putting my future on the line.

To my amazement Olga showed no signs of shock or disbelief but listened intently, warmly, and finally said, "Ambrose, I too have these experiences. I too see people from the other world. And I also have been used in healing."

It was a strange turn for both of us. In dealing with others, both Olga and I could often cross the bridge of time into the past, even into the future. Yet we had had no glimmering of the truth about ourselves.

None of it mattered, of course, the world was ahead of us, the world to conquer; we were young, in love, concerned with ourselves and our future.

I had to explain to her that our company, the Glenn L. Martin Company, was opening a large new plant near Baltimore, and I was assigned to help open the plant and to remain there in Baltimore. So we would be moving within a few months after we were married. To Olga this meant uprooting her whole life, tearing herself from her family and her home.

There was so much she did not know about me or the world of England that I had come from, just as I knew so little about her life and her world.

It was long after we were married before Olga told me the story of the knockings of the bedroom wall and in the furniture.

When she did tell me, I said to her, "Olga, that was going on just about the time you and I met, just before Christmas. Why didn't you speak of it to me after you realized my own interest in these things?"

Olga smiled the special smile women reserve for moments of wisdom and superiority. "There simply wasn't any reason to speak of it, dear."

"What do you mean?" I demanded. "No reason!"

"But the knockings stopped, Ambrose," Olga explained with infinite patience. "They stopped and haven't been heard again. Not since the night you and I met—the night of that party in my home."

8 ᓚ Bride

Olga herself has written down, from her memories and notes on early experiences, her record of what her early youth was like. I would like to quote Olga here in her own words:

"By the time I was three years old it became very apparent to my parents that they did indeed have a child with a frightening and undesirable trait that caused her to claim the ability to see and hear those who had died. . . .

"To further complicate matters I would describe people whom my parents had known in the old country and who, unknown to my parents, had died. These phenomena greatly disturbed my parents. . . . I was the one child of the eleven who saw things that no one else could see, and made prophecies that were laughed at, but that came to pass, much to their consternation and alarm.

"My visions of discarnate entities caused father to have Mass said so that these departed souls could rest in peace, but they continued to appear to me and did not seem to be unpeaceful in these appearances. Candles were burned and prayers offered to free me from this disturbing and even embarrassing peculiarity. But instead of release, this gift only appeared to be developing more strongly and with greater meaning.

"After a time my parents decided that there was nothing they could do to change me or to get rid of these aberrations and notions of seeing things at night. They accepted me for what I was to them—an enigma. And they gave me love and all the understanding and patience they could give.

"No child—sensitively gifted or not—could ask for more!"

Although Olga was born in Cleveland, both her parents had been born abroad, of distinguished, even noble ancestry. Her mother, Elizabeth Mary Karanczay, born in Hungary, was a great-granddaughter of Hungary's famous general, Joseph Karanczay. Her mother's father, Count Joseph Karanczay, had been court interpreter for Emperor Franz Joseph. He spoke twenty-three languages. Olga's mother spoke seven languages fluently. Olga's father was a Russian theologian whose ancestors had migrated from Moscow to Carpathia. They were married in Hungary, but a year after the marriage the Russian Czar ordered Olga's father to go to America to organize Russian Orthodox parishes throughout the eastern United States. Olga's mother refused to accompany him on the grounds that America was a wilderness where Indians roamed with bow and arrows and she was not about to be scalped. So he made the journey alone on a sailing vessel.

Once he reached America he realized that this was in truth the promised land, and he wrote back to tell Olga's mother that she and their son, first born of this large family-to-be, should come at once to America. Elizabeth agreed to come, but only if her father accompanied her, as well as the infant offspring and the nursemaid.

Olga's father had been educated in Russia for the priesthood in the Russian Orthodox Church. Since her mother was a Roman Catholic, her father had to pay a fine to the Russian Church which would have amounted in American money to fifty dollars. This was a source of humor in the family—and an item the father occasionally injected into the course of a discussion or difference of opinion.

Differences in religion did play a minor role in their lives. Olga's parents were married at a High Mass in the Roman Catholic Church. They were married by Olga's great-uncle who was a Roman Catholic Bishop. When the first child came, a dilemma arose. Was he to be christened in the Russian Orthodox Church of his father's, or in the Roman Catholic faith? It was Olga's Catholic uncle, the Bishop, who ruled that for the good of all concerned the son was to be christened in his father's church, and moreover that all of their children should be christened in the father's faith. There was a total of seventeen children born of this marriage. All were christened in the Russian Orthodox ritual.

Olga was taken by her mother to be "churched," a ceremony observed in the Orthodox religion forty days after the infant's birth. From that time on she was brought to church regularly. For the first few years she was carried in her mother's arms. After that she stood. In the old Orthodox Church everyone stood throughout the service. There were no pews. When she was five, Olga stood with the other children in long lines, one behind the other, and no playing or fooling or talking; any of these would have meant a pulled ear and then a spanking at home! She learned to polish her penny, as the other children did, on the coat of the child in front of her. (One had to wet the rim of the penny to make it shine.) There was a good deal of standing and kneeling and standing; sometimes the boy or girl behind her would twist her shoe and try to make her fall over as she knelt. They were typical children, in and out of church.

Olga's early years were truly a period of learning, love, laughter, and discipline. Mostly discipline. Her teachers were instructed by her parents to be severe. "You are her mother while you are teaching her," the parents would tell the teacher. "If she misbehaves, spank her. And tell us and we will do the same." Fortunately, this discipline was never administered; Olga knew better than to invite this correction. She went to public school from eight thirty in the morning to three thirty in the afternoon, learning all the things as seen through the eyes of American schools and teachers. From four to six she attended with other Russian Orthodox children the Russian Orthodox School, where they were taught to read and write and speak the Russian language as well as Slavonic, the language of the Church. They were told that they had to learn to speak this language well, for this was the language spoken in heaven by the saints.

As in any large family, there were chores to do, helping the laundress empty the tubs, turning the clothes wringer, bringing in coal and wood for the fireplaces, baby-sitting—all the chores of the past, now, unfortunately, too often forgotten. They were a big, delightful, noisy, boisterous family, a flock of normal kids growing up in a home of normal parents, arguments, disputes, battles, joys, and loves.

It was at the age of three that she began to have the same kind of episodes I had as a boy—the clairvoyance of early childhood, seeing people in her room in the dark and not understanding what or who they were.

This is an experience that has happened to other "sensitives" as children. Episodes are usually difficult and emotionally disruptive for both child and parent because so often the parent has no idea what is happening; he tries to tell the child that it is all his imagination, or that he is merely making things up to attract attention, or that he is mentally ill and should see a doctor. He is told, in the kindest way, that no one is there, in any case; or that it is something frightening and bad and the child becomes terrified of the dark. None of this is the parents' fault; they simply do not know how to react to the psychic child; it is a part of our education that has yet to be understood and developed.

Because of this, many sensitives as children are put through needless anguish by well-meaning adults who do not understand.

One episode in Olga's very early childhood caused great upheaval both in her family and in her attitude. Curiously, this was an experience very similar to one experienced in my own youth, although in Olga's case it occurred at a much younger age.

Olga was only ten years old when her mother gave birth to her last child, a son. The infant appeared to be normal and in good health. Six months later Olga received a psychic impression that the infant was to die, that he was to leave his body and join the beings in the world on the other side.

Olga, with much joy, announced to her older brothers that the baby brother was going to die.

I must reiterate that in her young mind the child was not dying in the sense that the world thinks of death, but only passing on to another, even happier state.

The reaction was not what she had anticipated. Her brothers looked at her with horror. They knew her statements in the past often were borne out by later events. They hurried to their mother.

Greatly alarmed, her mother called Olga in. What led her to make such a stupid, foolish statement? Olga replied, "But it is true. He is going to leave his body."

Olga's mother turned her over her knee and whipped her. She told Olga never to say such a terrible thing again, or anything like it. There were to be no more predictions. And no more stories about the dead people, and no more waking up mother at all hours to tell her that "they"—the people Olga saw—were back again, standing by her bed.

One of these people Olga sees is a sister named Margaret, who died before Olga was born and with whom Olga became friends across the invisible barriers.

To her, what she heard, what she saw, was real and immediate and undeniable. Why could she see and know these things that others could not see or hear? Sincerely religious, Olga wondered if she had in some way unknown to her committed a terrible sin for which God now was punishing her.

To climax these growing fears, three days after her prediction her infant brother died.

The terrible fact that she had predicted this thing, when the baby had appeared completely well, bothered her most. Had she been responsible in some psychic way merely by saying the words?

The condition which brought on the infant's sudden death proved to be on investigation a congenital heart impairment that had not been discovered but that had made death of the infant almost inevitable within days or weeks. No one had known about this condition. Ten-year-old Olga simply received the information through clairvoyant vision.

Olga saw her parents, her family, grief-stricken about her brother's death, and she knew even if they did not say so, they remembered her prediction. She had done nothing wrong, but she began to suspect that her visions and prophecies were dangerous, that they were to be avoided. She would guard against telling people what she saw; she would keep still when the prediction or the impulse to make a prediction strove to take over.

The darkness during these early years was haunted by those unwelcome visitors. Her mother had told her strongly *not* to awaken her any more, and Olga had promised she would obey.

"At night," Olga was to recall to me, "when the lights were out in my bedroom, put out by my mother, never by me, I would cover my head with the sheet or blanket because I did not want to have to look into that darkness. I knew what I would see."

Neither her parents nor her brothers and sisters ever realized how unhappy they had made her by their lack of understanding. She had learned, as I learned, to keep quiet about these things because it was so hard for others to understand.

Nevertheless, she continued to have these experiences. She could see people's auras, emanations in various colors around a person, sometimes gold or white, sometimes blue, sometimes, when the individual was in anger or despair, red or deep brown verging into black or blue-black.

The first aura she was to see, in fact, was her own. As she relates this, she was perhaps five or six years old, and would climb upon a chair and look at herself in a large mirror with an elaborate gilded frame. This mirror hung between two windows in the front parlor of her family's home in Cleveland. Olga was always careful to do this when she was sure no one was around. She would push a chair in front of the mirror, stand on the chair, and gaze into the mirror at herself and her aura. She did not call it her aura because she had never heard the word. To Olga she was looking at her "ghost." That was what she called these colored emanations that ran like a nimbus around her reflection.

After her infant brother's death, a change came over her. "I didn't want to look in the mirror again at my ghost," Olga related. "I was frightened because there is in Russia—in old Russia— a superstition that after someone dies it is bad luck to look into a mirror because you may see the face of the dead reflected beside you.

After her prediction and the infant's death, she had come to feel that all of this was undesirable; and she wanted to stay as far from these things as she could. She was literally afraid now of all these experiences.

One day, several years later, her fears had receded to a point where she decided to look again into this mirror with the gilded frame. But she saw no sign of her "ghost" in the looking glass. Perhaps the fact that she had not looked for all these years had something to do with it; perhaps these are gifts that die if unused.

In any case Olga to this writing has not seen her own aura again in the glass. Occasionally, particularly in healing situations, she does see auras around other individuals.

The healing flow began with Olga very early. Olga cannot recall when it first began; perhaps it was as early as when she started to see figures in the dark. Perhaps it began, as I think most likely, by her small childish hands reaching out with the fingers of child love to touch someone—when her mother or a sister or brother or some neighbor complained of a headache or a pain in her arm or something of that sort.

To Olga it was a natural, almost unconscious gesture: *I will make it well, I will touch it and make it well.* She did not really say the words, yet in effect this was what she was saying with her hands. And her mother, to her surprise, would discover that her headache had gone. So she would say, "Olga, come and put your hand on my forehead. I have a headache." Olga would do this without thought that it was anything unusual.

One day her mother called her for something more serious. Busy with the household, unable to leave the children or the home often for more than a few minutes or hours, her mother rarely bothered with physical checkups. For months she had had some pain in her abdomen; eventually she went to the doctor who informed her that she had a floating kidney and required an operation before the condition grew more serious.

The mother had no time for such things. There were too many other demands. The condition—and the pain—grew worse. One day, lying on her bed in severe pain, the mother spoke to Olga. "You've healed my headaches," she said. "Put your hands on my back and make it well."

Olga put her hand on the spot where her mother indicated there was pain, and she said a small prayer, "Dear God, please heal my mummy. Thank you, Jesus. Amen."

That was all. Nor did she have any idea where or how this prayer took shape; it was the natural, simple, unstudied petition of a child.

Yet, almost instantly, the mother's pain began to subside. In five minutes it was completely gone. The kidney condition never returned. She lived for many years after that, until Olga was a grown woman. When she died she was in her seventy-ninth year.

This story spread quickly in the neighborhood. It was not long before little Olga was known for the fact that there was some quality of healing in her hands. Not infrequently a neighbor would send a son or a daughter to the house to ask if Olga would come, mother has a backache. Could Olga just come and rub her back a little?

In one instance a call of this kind involved Olga—still a young girl—in a critical situation. She had no knowledge of what was wrong. Yet not to act could have cost a woman's life. It was as if a little girl with no medical knowledge whatsoever were given not only diagnosis but also therapeutic procedures, psychic or extrasensory communication.

A boy from across the street ran into the Ripich home and cried out, "Baba, Baba!" In Russian this means "grandma," which is what all the children called Olga's mother. The excited child went on, "My mummy cut herself and she is dying. Come over quick."

Olga's mother told Olga to go over and see what was wrong and she in the meantime would call the doctor. When Olga entered the home across the street, looking for the mother, she heard a moaning coming from the bathroom. Hurrying into the bathroom, she found the boy's mother lying unconscious on the floor, in a pool of blood.

Olga had never heard of a miscarriage. She had no medical knowledge. But she realized that this woman was bleeding to death and something had to be done. The doctor would come but it would be too late.

What she did was entirely automatic. In this moment as if she knew what to do, without knowing how she knew, she dragged the woman out of this pool of blood into the bedroom, got her onto the bed. There she obtained and carefully placed under the woman's hips a pillow.

She then ran into the kitchen, opened the ice box, and brought back into the bedroom a large piece of ice, put it in a towel, and placed it upon the woman's abdomen.

By that time the doctor had arrived. When he saw the woman he said to Olga, "Where's the nurse?"

"What nurse?" Olga asked.

"The one who took care of her."

"I took care of her," Olga said.

Surprised, the doctor asked, "Who told you what to do?"

Olga said, "I don't know. I just knew."

And he said, "Do you realize that you saved her life?"

He immediately called an ambulance and sent her off to a hospital. The woman recovered.

By positioning the pillow and the ice correctly she had halted the outgushing flow of blood that would almost certainly have brought on the woman's death before the doctor could have arrived.

When she was nineteen, a girl chum of Olga's met her at the office and suggested that they go to East Cleveland to see a woman who could, the girl said, "tell what you think." By that she meant that the woman for a fifty-cent fee could look at you and tell you all things past, present, and future.

Olga explained that she didn't have fifty cents with her; besides, if she went along she would have to telephone her mother to let her know where she would be. She did call, and her mother was furious. She didn't want Olga to have any readings or anything like a reading. "Stay away from that woman."

Olga assured her she couldn't be hurt because she couldn't possibly have a reading. "I don't have the money. I'll just tag along with Mary, that's all."

On these conditions her mother relented. But Olga was to have nothing personally to do with the woman.

When they arrived, however, the woman took one look at Olga and announced to the other girl, "I'm not interested in you today. I want to talk with this girl."

Olga said, "I can't. I don't have fifty cents to pay you."

The woman said, "I don't want any money."

She took Olga into a room and proceeded to tell Olga all about herself, her family, and her background. Olga remembered the warnings of her mother. She said to herself as she sat in the rocking chair, "There's nothing to this."

The woman said, as if reading this out of Olga's mind, "Don't think that kind of thought." Then the woman declared that Olga was going to marry a man from the old country. "He knows you but you have never met him on earth. His name I can't get—his initial is A. You will marry this man and you will go to live in a city whose initial is B." Then she added, "You are one of us and you are going to be doing what I am doing." At this point she informed Olga that she herself came from Vienna, where she had worked for her government during the war as a medium and was pensioned by the government and sent to America to live.

She also said that Olga's sister-in-law would have a baby, that she would be ill after the birth of the baby, and that Olga would take care of the infant during this illness but that the sister-in-law would eventually recover.

On Olga's arrival home her mother ordered her to "march right upstairs to your bedroom, young lady, and don't you dare tell your father where you have been."

There were guests coming that night, but Olga had to stay in her room. When the guests left, her mother came in, closed the door, and said, "Now tell me, what did that woman say?"

Olga related all that was said. Her mother was amazed because many things Olga had not known, the mother knew to be true. What the woman had told Olga about the family was absolutely accurate.

The prediction that Olga's sister-in-law would have her child and be ill for some time afterward developed exactly as the woman had foretold. About a month after she had her baby boy, she became ill and had to be hospitalized. She was in the hospital for eight months. Olga gave up her secretarial job in order to take care of the infant in this emergency.

Eight months later the doctor told Olga's brother to take his wife home. The doctor felt that Olga and her mother could heal his wife. The wife came into the home and Olga nursed her. By the time the baby was thirteen months old the wife was well enough to take care of the child herself.

This reading by the woman was extraordinary in its accuracy not only of the past but equally of the future. The woman even described to Olga what I looked like, the color of my hair—a color photograph of the future in sharp clear focus.

And all of that was two years before the knockings came on the wall and in the furniture of Olga's bedroom in the Christmas season of 1927.

After we had revealed to each other our mutual interest in psychic phenomena, I discussed with Olga many of the ideas and theories I had read or studied in this field. Despite her various experiences, Olga had never read of these things at all. I gave her a book about spiritualism—the first time she had ever heard the word "spiritualism"—to help her understand what she had been experiencing. We discussed many phases of psychic phenomena, even astral flight. Olga was interested but cautious. Could it really be done? I told her, "After I leave here tonight, I will return to your room and you will know it. I will prove to you that I can travel in this way."

Later that night Olga was in bed. Because her father was ill, her mother was sleeping that night with Olga. After they were in bed and the light was out, the astral projection succeeded. I was there in the room. I tried to touch her but couldn't seem able to do so. I was close to her with my head against her and she looked down and saw me and cried out, "I see you, I see you."

Her mother, half asleep, awakened and said, "What are you mumbling about?"

Olga said, "I guess I was just dreaming."

But the next night when I told her I had come into her room by this psychic journey, she said, "I saw you, I saw you."

The words and the repetition paraphrased in past tense what I had heard her say in the room.

She told me further that she had not only heard me and seen me, but actually felt my presence.

It was Olga, however, who demonstrated a remarkable ability in this form of psychic teleportation. She herself has written of this personal experiment in her notes:

"After Ambrose left me that night, and I had gone to bed, I found myself in his bedroom. I remember standing by his bedside, looking down at him. The next night he came to see me and then told me that I had awakened him and held in my hand crushed glass. This was significant because—although nothing had been broken—he had fallen asleep with his glasses on and I was worried that he might break them while he slept. . . ."

Also evidential was the fact that Olga described in detail my room, although she had never been there personally and I had never given her any description of it.

We were married on June 7, 1928, in the Russian Orthodox Church of St. Theodosius. The wedding took place at six o'clock in the evening, in a very colorful candlelit service. Most of the service was in Russian, and I have often mentioned to Olga that I never could be absolutely sure that we were really married because I understood so little of what was said. Olga's father participated, along with her brother-in-law, the Very Rt. Rev. Joseph Dzvonchik, husband of Olga's oldest sister, and the Russian Orthodox priest who had baptized Olga and was almost like a second father, the Very Rt. Rev. Jason Kappanadze. The service took over an hour.

The wedding was very beautiful. As a Methodist I was not too familiar with all of that color and pageantry. Both Olga's father and the family priest told Olga to follow the religion of her husband, as Olga's mother had done—but never to forget the Russian Orthodox Church. Olga has always carried out this injunction. She sometimes describes herself as a Russian Orthodox Methodist.

There was a large and wonderful reception in Olga's home. Her mother served a banquet to two hundred and fifty guests. There were long tables, flowers, and rare foods. The wedding cake was so large it took two men to carry it in.

Olga and I had to eat from one plate all through this celebration and, in accordance with an old world custom, every time someone tapped his water glass, Olga and I had to kiss in order to sweeten the food, as they put it.

9 ঌ Unfoldment

I told Olga I regretted that the lack of finances prevented me from providing her with an elaborate out-of-town honeymoon, but Olga said our whole life would be her honeymoon. Which was reassuring to me.

Not too reassuring, however, as we set out on this matrimonial journey of our lives, was our first apartment. To our dismay we discovered that it was infested with unpleasant forces, what some call poltergeist—unenlightened discarnate beings that take over.

This was a four-and-a-half room apartment in a red-brick, two-story apartment house that had a total of sixteen apartments, a pleasant-looking building not too far from our Cleveland plant. But there were noises, there were door slammings, a window would crash down. Things that had no apparent physical reason for happening—happened. A light would be on when the switch was turned to the off position—and would be on when the switch was pressed to the on position. Then it would be switched off. A pantry door that had to be pried open with a screwdriver would fly open with a terrible clatter with the lights off. We were to find out that a former tenant had died here and no tenant was able to stay more than a few weeks.

Had this occurred only once or twice, or even a half dozen times, we might have thought it was merely imagination, but the happenings kept on, and Olga, for the first time in her life away from her home, alone in the apartment long hours during the day and at night while I was at work and at school, was uneasy.

I decided to try a variation of an experiment I had done with my friend in England: writing down the alphabet on a large piece of paper and placing a tumbler over it, upside down. On this tumbler both Olga and I put our hands.

Olga had never seen such an experiment before, but we went ahead with it. A message came through to us that we were to find another apartment. We were given a street, East 173rd Street in Cleveland, near St. Clair. The tumbler spelled out that we would get an apartment there for thirty-five dollars a month. This was five dollars less than we were paying for our haunted four-and-a-half rooms.

We had to look up the address and find out how to get there. When we reached the street there was one building with a sign out: *Apartment for Rent*. The people were Polish-Ukranians, very pleasant and friendly. The young owner said the rent was forty dollars a month.

I looked at Olga because this was not what the message had spelled out. At the same moment, a brother of the owner called out, "Do you two have any children?"

"No, none," we told him.

"In that case," the brother volunteered, "let's give them a break. Make it thirty-five dollars."

We rented the apartment that day and moved out of the other apartment the following week.

In the new place all was peaceful. We could begin our new lives together with an aura of happiness.

Before Olga and I met, however, I often attended parties sponsored by members of the Order of St. George, an organization of persons who had come here from England. Dances and parties were held in homes of members. It was a pleasant experience; we were all young, full of ideas and goals in this new land to which we had come, as twentieth-century pilgrims, in search of ourselves and the future.

One night at one of these parties of the Order of St. George, I glanced at my hostess and noticed behind her what looked like a large dark cloud sweeping through the wall of the house. It appeared to hover over the head of my hostess. At the same moment, I saw the hostess put her hand to her forehead as if in pain. I also saw the face of another woman in the cloud. I did not quite know what to do, but as the look of pain remained on her face, I went to my hostess and asked if anything were wrong. She said no, it was only that she had a terrible headache.

I said to her, "I see a woman near you."

I described the woman I saw in this cloud above her. I asked if she happened to know the woman.

She said, "I certainly do. She is a neighbor of mine."

"Have you any idea why she is sending you a headache?"

She seemed startled by all of this but said, "Yes. We had a slight disagreement and frankly I didn't invite her to this party."

"She is sending you a destructive thought or thoughts and you are accepting them. Now that you realize it, you must not allow them to enter."

Once she understood that she had to reject this mental assault, the pain left her.

This entire incident was taking place while others were listening. They heard me describe to the hostess the dark cloud I saw above her head and the face of the woman. They heard the woman's recognition of her neighbor in my description, and her explanation of the animosity.

They also heard her state, quite suddenly and with some surprise after she had been made to realize what was happening, that the pain was gone.

There was much buzzing about this incident. Many guests began to question me about my interest in this area. I quickly explained that though I had psychic gifts, I did not use them for any material purposes. One young man asked me if I ever did any healing or knew about it. I told him I had done some in England.

He told me his name was Tom Middlebrook and asked me to meet his wife, Anne, a beautiful girl who had been seriously ill much of her life. She had been brought up in England and developed a rheumatic heart condition. She had also developed a goiter. Moreover, she had a swollen condition in her knees that was causing extreme pain. She was, indeed, a very ill woman. Her husband said to me, "We wonder, if there's anything *you* could do for Anne? The doctors don't seem able to do a thing to help. She lives in pain."

I knelt beside the woman. Her knees were badly swollen. I had learned by that time that the force of healing came—as does all psychic force—only by relaxing, by allowing oneself to be used by the force, not to strain, not to reach out, not to make effort at all.

I allowed myself to relax. I sought only to become one with the wave length of the woman. Both patient and healer should be in a kind of concord and this is achieved by "tuning in." Each healer, let me state, must act in accordance with his guidance; not all are alike in approach or in method.

After some moments of reaching out to form a psychic oneness with Anne, and feeling that this had been achieved, I put my hands on the swollen knees. I do not know precisely how long I held them. It could have been half a minute, even a whole minute.

As I drew my fingers away, I heard Tom say, "Look—your hands —they've turned black."

I looked down and saw that it was true: both hands seemed to have absorbed something, some of the dark infected coloration of the knees; they had taken on the black stormy hue.

Without knowing what directed me to do it, I stood up and shook my hands exactly as one shakes off some foreign substance, water or oil or soil. I literally shook off that blackness on my hands, whatever it was. The blackness was gone in that instant. My hands were again their normal fleshtone.

At the same moment, I heard Anne say, "Look—my knees—the swelling is almost down. The pain is gone."

It was true. The swelling was actually gone within a matter of minutes. It was a curious, unbelievable moment for all of us, including myself.

After Olga and I were married, she came to know the Middlebrooks too; they were among our closest friends, and indeed I gave Mrs. Middlebrook many treatments over many years. A few years later, after we moved to Baltimore, they came too. The depression was at its height, and I helped Tom obtain a new post there in business. His wife took treatments at Johns Hopkins. The doctors were amazed that she was still alive because she had been taking, on doctor's orders, massive doses of digitalis, doses far in excess of what she should have been taking, in their opinion.

Of course, neither my wife nor I had anything to do with the administration of medicines. All we did was our own forms of prayer and spiritual therapy which we—and the Middlebrooks—believed were helpful. And which, much to the amazement of doctors in this case, kept Mrs. Middlebrook alive for many years, long enough for the couple's only child to get to know her mother.

In December, 1928, six months after my marriage, we left for Baltimore, where the new Glenn L. Martin plant was about to be built at Middle River on the Baltimore outskirts.

But the vast Middle River plant was not even yet a full-fledged blueprint as we set out. Heading from Cleveland to Baltimore, we drove in a new Oldsmobile over roads far different from the modern thruways. Olga was pregnant, but the doctors had assured us things were sufficiently along that there was no danger in taking the trip. Nevertheless, the roads were twisting, narrow, and over the Pennsylvania mountains we ran into storms; the road was curving and in many places the sides were steep and unprotected, plunging down hundreds of feet. I remember one moment when things looked dark on this trip and I asked Olga, "Are you frightened?"

Her answer I will never forget. She said, "I am never frightened when you are with me."

That trust and tenderness has always been to me the heart of our marriage, capable of riding out any storm, joy—or tragedy—that lay ahead.

As soon as we reached Baltimore, we had to find a place to live and I had to go to work. The company was operating in temporary quarters in rented warehouses of the Colgate Company. In those warehouses I started an assembly department which consisted of a staff of one man—myself. Gradually we began to hire people and set up work on a special assignment: building a plane, the XT5M. We got the fuselage department in operation in these temporary quarters; also, I was the foreman of the fuselage department.

We rented a pleasant brown-shingled frame house in an area where all the houses were alike. On one occasion I walked right into the house next door and was about to kiss my wife when I realized it wasn't my kitchen at all—or my wife either.

To me at least this is simply one more demonstration that our psychic or intuitional talents are of no real value or meaning in such earthbound situations.

When the new plant began to go into construction, my work load increased considerably. I had the job of designing and laying out the shops in the new building, such as the machineshop, the cleaning and plating department which included designing the plating tanks, with their steamheating coils, electrical installations, and platforms; I had to design and lay out the cafeteria, including the ovens and sinks, the maintenance shop and the sheet metal department with its machines; it took long hours of toil at the plant. And Olga was pregnant and alone.

On the 10th of June, 1929, one month ahead of time, Olga gave birth to twins. These were two of the most handsome children in the world, these infants we loved so much. But the house we lived in seemed too cramped, and the basement flooded frequently when it rained, and the dampness seemed to indicate we ought to move. We took another house.

The doctor prescribed a change in milk formula for the twins in the month of August. My wife protested against the change, but the doctor insisted it had to be made. The twins became ill with diarrhea and a week later, the younger was dead. Three days after that, the other boy also passed on in spite of the efforts of a baby specialist called in on the case. My wife Olga told me that she saw the spirit leave the little body in each case. "We had to release these children and give them back to God," my wife said, and these words she has repeated many times.

I am sure that our grief at this loss can be understood by any parent. Nor could there be any denial of our own personal deep-down sense of resentment at this time. We did not give up these two children willingly, joyfully, and it would be a lie to say otherwise. We are simple human beings; we love as others love, we grieve as others grieve.

It took perhaps as long as a year before we were fully adjusted, before we could completely understand that these children were not lost, really, that they were still ours, that we shared them in another way, at another level of existence and reality.

But immediately after their death we felt only bitter pain at this loss. Olga would not enter again the house where they died. The movers went in and took out all our belongings and transported them to a new house into which we moved.

One night, shortly after we had moved into our new home, something happened which was of incalculable significance to us in changing and indeed washing away the terrible despondency which had gripped both of us during those almost unbearable weeks.

As we were going to sleep, I felt the presence of something, or someone, in the room. It was visible in a kind of glow in the darkness.

As I lay there, wondering what it was, and knowing, without knowing how, that it was not something about which to be disturbed, my wife said to me, "Do you see it, dear? Do you see her?"

She began to describe what to me was no more than a fusion of light and shadows. To her the details were all revealed precisely. And, as she described the woman, I told her, "This is Edith—my sister Edith."

Olga said, "She is holding something, Ambrose. She is holding our children in her arms. She is saying that they are happy—and in her care!"

I know how difficult it must be for the average person to accept this. We must each see and understand as we are given to see and understand. But I can point out how difficult it is even now to write of these things. How deeply it stirs us to speak of them.

Perhaps, also, realizing our grief at this tragedy, one can imagine how much that night must have meant to us, when, for the first time, as was to happen many times after that, we saw before us—in the shadows of our room—those children whom we loved so much.

It was through them that we found our way into the ministry of healing which began for us with other children in pain, in need of succor.

Both Olga and I came to realize that we were not capable of living for ourselves alone, for our own goals alone. Psychic gifts of this sort could not be hidden; the special talents we seemed to have were for a purpose, for God's purpose.

"But in what direction do we go with these gifts?" Olga asked. "You've done this over the years. I haven't. How do we use this force? We aren't doctors."

"Of course we're not, but I have my work and career at Martin's and I'm going to follow that, because whatever we do with these spiritual powers, it must be done freely, given without charge, to those who need our help."

This was our pact with ourselves.

10 ❧ Rebirth

Seated beside us at a lecture we were attending in Baltimore on comparative religion was a well-dressed man who had an air of great concern and worry. During the evening, he introduced himself to us. He was, he explained, the manager of a large produce firm.

When he heard our name, he became quite excited; he had heard of my psychic investigations through a group interested in metaphysical research. After the meeting he asked me, "Could I call on you for help?"

He called several times when I was out. He told Olga he had to talk with me. It was life or death, and it was about his little girl. He told Olga, "I have a desperately ill daughter. Two of my children have already died of the same disease. The doctor says he can do nothing. Will your husband try to help her?"

The statement that he had lost two children could not fail to touch Olga with special personal meaning. We also had lost two children. His battle to save the third, even though the physician said no more could be done, struck an echo in Olga's heart.

Olga said she would talk to me and would he call later. When he called about six that evening, I told him, "Bring your daughter to our home tonight, and I will look at her and see what I can do."

He said he could not do that; the girl was too ill. Wouldn't we please come to them to see her?

I agreed. Olga and I went together to this man's home. The child was six years old. She was not able to go to school. An extremely pallid, fragile-looking child, she had weighed forty-two pounds for two years. We saw this little girl walking around the house while we were there.

Regarding the medical diagnosis, the father explained that she had a constrictive heart disease. The doctor had told the father that nothing could be done to alleviate or arrest the condition of the third child. He explained that this caused the death of the other two children. "Keep her happy—at any price"—those were the doctor's specific instructions. The only recourse left to the parents was to make her as comfortable as possible, give her all the candy she could eat, and wait for her to die.

When I saw this little girl, I realized that she could go out on her own and I told the father so. I said I wanted to treat her at my home. I felt she was strong enough to do this. He agreed. My purpose was not merely to make it easier for me. I wanted to work with her in a new atmosphere.

While at the house I gave the child a "treatment" through the laying on of hands, and I instructed the parents to bring her to our home later in the week.

That night I took her into an upstairs room that our godchild Doreen had named "the healing room" and where we had set up a special table. The child tired very easily; I wanted her in a restful position.

I placed my hands on her back. For the most part I simply let my hands rest there, motionless, one on the shoulder blade, one near the small of her back. I did a little massaging of her neck. Nothing dramatic, nothing emotional, everything calm, quiet.

After a little time I knew that the treatment was over, and I asked the parents to bring her back to me in a week.

There was no dramatic instantaneous healing, no sensation of force pouring out to heal her. Yet she seemed happier, stronger, after that first treatment. And she returned for further treatments. Each week the change became more and more noticeable.

Each case is different. I can't state precisely what I do in any given treatment. I know I did not consciously direct a force of healing to her; rather this was a technique of waiting, a sympathy that was not sympathy as we understand that word so much as a deep outreaching, continuing, and growing compassion. But all the time I directed my thinking and feeling to the idea of quiet waiting, quiet certainty for this six year old.

She began to get better. This was the fact that must be considered above everything else. The doctor had said he could do no more, that she would not get better. *But she did get better.* Whatever she had—whatever disease it was that the doctor said brought death to her sister and brother—she did not die from. She began to gain weight, which she had not done for two years. She began to show signs of renewal of strength, of energy. Within a few months, she was well enough to go back to school.

When the doctor who told the parents to give her candy and wait for her to die examined her, he could find no further trace of heart disease and he could find no explanation of what had cured the disease. Other doctors examining her confirmed this view. Several years later chest x-rays taken in a routine family checkup disclosed that she had had tuberculosis in a severe state in addition to the heart condition, but this too had been cured; the lesions were entirely healed.

I am not attempting here to give either a medical diagnosis or an explanation. What we had was a six-year-old girl who had not gained a pound in two years, who was obviously in a serious, almost critical condition when I first saw her, whose own physician had given her up as a terminal case. This was the child whom they brought to us. This was the child we treated by the techniques of spiritual therapy, with no other additional factors brought in beyond these treatments. This child who the doctor said couldn't improve, progressed from sickness to complete wholeness.

That was our first major case with a child. It was many, many years ago. The little girl of six years—as I write of this—is now a woman in her thirties, happily married. She has had no recurrence of that childhood affliction in all these years.

We began to get other calls for help.

Not long after the case of this girl Olga was riding into town on a streetcar. A neighbor she knew slightly sat down beside her.

As if she had sat there for this purpose, the neighbor began to talk about her eight-year-old son who was ill with a heart condition. He was unable to gain weight and almost unable to walk. Olga told her that sometimes her husband could help little children and that if she were at all interested she could bring the child to her husband.

The woman said she had heard about Mr. Worrall and had often thought of asking if she could come to see him with her son, but she had not wanted to impose on him. Olga told her by all means to bring the boy that night.

He was a thin, pinched-faced little lad called Bobby. I administered the laying on of hands for this boy, as I had with the little girl. At this time I had reached a point in my study of psychic healing and truth—quite apart from my work in science and aeronautics—where I did not consciously have to reach out with prayer or controlled meditation. With children especially, I found it very easy to relax. Not only are children the repositories of infinite possibilities, but they also have within them still the murmur of angel wings, an essence of divinity, unscathed. With adults, even in healing situations, I have often felt unspoken challenge—faith that too often equivocates, questions, rejects.

With children it is different. They believe. They accept. They do not doubt in the terms of adult doubt. They wait upon the spirit in the fullness of their child wonder, their faith, their acceptance; their innocence opens the gateway of faith—and healing.

Bobby began to have the same reactions as the little girl I had treated. He grew stronger, the heart condition disappeared. He gained weight; he was soon attending school. Eventually, Bobby fully recovered. In fact, one day I received a message from him: "I'm going to take up tap dancing. The doctors say it's okay."

He became a well-known amateur dancer, appearing at parties and club functions.

People, hearing of our work, were calling or writing, asking for help, all kinds of help for every kind of trouble—medical, physical, mental, emotional. They were bringing their sick for healing to our front door. Because I was busy at my work in the aircraft company, eight to ten hours a day, all of this had to be done after hours in the evening.

The question of payment arose seriously as soon as these people began to arrive in such numbers that there would be several waiting at a time during the evening. A woman on leaving, weeping in happiness because a severe back difficulty had been corrected, asked Olga, "How much do I owe for this?"

Olga's decision, and mine, was quite simple. Her impulsive and instinctive answer, which has never changed, was simply, "We don't charge anything and we don't accept anything. If you yourself want to give something to some organization or church or charity in gratitude to God, that is up to you. But you must do this yourself."

Sometimes a child would bring us a token gift, a flower pot or perhaps some jam made by the parents. Such things that have no monetary value at all we do accept rather than cause hurt. But that is the absolute limit.

In this period of beginnings the great majority of cases were children. I recall a boy who had what the physicians diagnosed as polio. Clairvoyantly, I became aware that it was not polio at all, but an accident of some kind involving the lad's bicycle. I taxed him with this fact and, startled that I knew, he admitted he had fallen from his bicycle and simply had been afraid to tell his parents what had happened. Once understood, it was a simple matter to deal with, indeed hardly more than a subluxation of a vertebra.

Another far more difficult and challenging case was a seven-year-old spastic of the most severe type. The boy could not go to school at all. He had an underdeveloped chin. His legs were in a permanent crossed position. His arms were crossed. His shoulder blades and shoulders were twisted at ninety-degree angles from their normal position in his body.

I agreed to work with this boy. We have never interfered with medical treatment; we insist physicians be consulted in all cases. We believe prayer and medicine do not stand unalterably opposed. We can work with doctors; we are not against them. Spiritual healing, like all healing, is only a technique for achieving wholeness and all wholeness is of God.

I began to use the same technique with this boy as I had on the other children, the laying on of hands, the certainty of God's love as revealed in the child, awareness of healing forces within myself and the child, awareness of currents that flow without conscious effort on my part.

Again the spectacular, the instantaneous, did not occur. This chinless little boy only gradually began to get better. He came to me in September. In two months' time the child was so improved that his father took the boy to school and asked that he be given another chance to attend classes like other children. The headmaster was informed that the boy was going regularly for spiritual treatments given by a man named Ambrose Worrall.

The headmaster had never heard of any Ambrose Worrall before, but he was a man of understanding and of love for children. He didn't know if this treatment would or would not work, but he did know that there was a great effort and love being poured out and he was willing to play his role, since there was already vast improvement evident. He would give the boy another chance in school.

Here was a case in which medicine could do no more but where other forces, the concern of this principal for his student, the concern of parent, of ourselves, the desire and instinctive longing of this boy for his rightful role in the world around him—all played a part.

It was not an easy case. But step by step the boy improved. His legs straightened, his arms straightened, he began to learn to speak properly. At our urging he was sent to one of the finest orthodontists in the city for a reconstruction of his teeth.

For three years he came to us for these treatments. He was indeed very much to us like a son, as dear to us as a son. He was graduated from grammar school and went on to high school. He even became a ball player. He walks straight, has a good job, talks well, he has a future before him.

There is an addenda to this story. One day while the boy's treatments were still going on, a business leader in the community rang the doorbell of the house where this boy lived. He told the father, "I pass by this house often. I've noticed your child, your boy. He's a spastic, isn't he?"

The father said yes, the boy was a spastic.

The man persisted, "But you're doing something—he's getting better, isn't he?"

The father asked, "Why is that important to you?"

The man then explained that he had a little girl who needed help. There was, according to all the medical people he had talked to, no hope that anything could be done to help her. She would spend her life this way, a hopeless homebound prisoner. The boy's father promised the man that he would ask Mr. Worrall to see his daughter.

She was fourteen years old at the time she was brought to me. A lovely girl—but the whole left side of her body was underdeveloped, she spoke only haltingly and was often too frightened to speak at all. She was subject to epileptic seizures. At the time of birth the mother had gone into a convulsion and, as a result, the child had suffered serious brain damage. A leading specialist in Baltimore to whom the child was taken for examination, stated that there was nothing that brain surgery could do to improve this situation.

This girl was truly a tragic case by the time she came to us. Because of the severity of her condition, I treated her three times a week for the first year, twice a week the second year, and once a week the third year. The doctor in this case, who saw her intermittently, asked after six months of this spiritual treatment,

"What are you doing? She is getting better. It is almost unbelievable."

The parents told him that they were bringing their daughter to me. The doctor said after a little, "I've heard of this sort of thing and I've heard of this man. All right. I don't know what it is—but keep right on doing it because it is a miracle."

She was improving, month by month. The left side of her body developed to match the right side. After the third year she was able to attend vocational school; she learned typing and got a regular office job. Through her social activities she met a young man who fell in love with her. They are now married and have grown children of their own. She has never had a recurrence of this ailment.

A whole new way of life was beginning. We did keep records; however, as time went on and more and more needed our help, this became so time-consuming that the letters from those who were healed were kept instead.

Healing did not—and does not—occur in every case. A child or adult may come with a tumor in advanced stages; despite all we do, the child dies. Is it our failure? Is it the unreversible process of life? Why does healing come in one instance and often, under identical circumstances on the surface, does not come in another?

The only answer to this, quite frankly and bluntly, is that we do not know. Neither do the physicians in many cases. There are many words and many theories and often many glib attempts at explanation, both for success in healing and for failure.

There are techniques, there are case histories, there are records that indicate healings. We understand why some are healed; we understand why some are not. But for the most part metaphysical healing is still in need of vast study and exploration.

We do know the following things:

Healings do occur—after physicians have given up, after full tests have been made, after all the records reveal that the patient does have a real, not imagined and not a so-called psychosomatic disorder or illness.

Mankind has made vast strides in medicine and surgery and these are also tools of God. But while we believe in the use of all the tools and instruments He provides, it is also true that the laws of health are little understood even today, particularly the effect of spiritual factors on health. Too few in healing reach out to the pool of health and well-being that is all around us, the infinite sea, as available to us as the air we breathe.

We do not understand how our psychic forces draw and replenish themselves from this source; we do not understand the psychic energy and chemistry within us and how it functions in terms of atoms and electrons and protons, in terms of concentrated energy and power. All of this remains to be explored; one day it may well change our entire attitude regarding health and sickness. We are only beginning to be aware of the intuitional forces.

One summer evening my friend, Tom Middlebrook, came to me for help. It was a stifling, breathless night. I was appalled as I saw the sight he presented. He had one great hive over his eye and several more on other parts of his face. He had one on his heel so big he could hardly walk; he had two on his legs that he had rubbed together and were bleeding. Others appeared all over his body.

He informed me that he had been going to Johns Hopkins about this condition and had been told that an operation might help, but results could not be guaranteed. His situation might remain the same or even grow worse, and it would cost many hundreds of dollars.

I sat down beside this man as he lay face downward on the table in the healing room. I waited. The impression I received was to place my thumb upon the left notch of his hip. So I placed my thumb there, pressing very lightly, and waited for perhaps another five minutes. Suddenly, he raised his head and said, "My, what a feeling."

"What do you feel, Tom?"

He said, "I feel all the fire going out of my hives."

I remained with my thumb on his hip for fifteen or twenty minutes longer. During this time all of the lumps disappeared as I sat waiting. He had no more sensation of heat or itching and, from that day on, he has never had any more hives.

Not long after this case Mrs. Myrtle Schwatka, mother of one of the children we had worked with, rang our doorbell at about five o'clock one afternoon. She was crying. She had just come from a surgeon's office and had been told that she would have to have her breast removed because a lump had been discovered.

She told Olga she wanted to see me before she allowed the operation to take place. She was to go into the hospital the following morning. She was a very large and heavy woman; the removal of a whole breast would have been not only very disfiguring, but undoubtedly dangerous.

Mrs. Schwatka worked in the manufacture of surgical garments and corsets; she was known to many physicians. Medicine, therefore, was a part of her life; she was not frightened of it by nature. But before she gave permission for the operation, she wanted me to treat her.

I arrived home from work only a few minutes after she came into the house. When she saw me she said, "Ambrose, heal this lump."

I told her to come up to the healing room and I would see what could be done.

She stood in the center of the room. I said to her, "Where is the lump?"

She took her hand and placed it on the lump on her breast. The lump was about the size of an egg. It was very bumpy and hard. I held this lump for a number of minutes in my hand and I felt no change taking place. I just stood there beside her for some minutes, relaxed, waiting for something to happen, some inspiration to come to direct me what to do.

Finally, after about five minutes, I received a strong impression to place my right hand on the back of her neck, while my left hand continued to hold the lump on her breast. After I placed my right hand on the back of her neck I felt the lump on her breast starting to reduce. I did not move but continued to stand there as before, relaxed, not saying anything. I knew the lump was shrinking in my hand. I could literally feel this shrinkage. I believe we must have stood like this for perhaps fifteen minutes. As this process went on, at the end of that time, the lump in her breast had shrunk to the size of a pea. By the time she got home, the lump had disappeared.

The next morning Mrs. Schwatka went to her doctor and asked him to re-examine her. The doctor said, "I examined it yesterday, Myrtle. That should be enough."

She said, "I still want you to look at it again."

He started to examine her and then asked her, "Where is it? What has happened? It was there yesterday"—a pause—"wasn't it, Myrtle?"

He insisted on knowing what had happened. She told him of her visit to me. The doctor said, "You're one lucky woman. I've heard of people who have that gift of healing. How fortunate you are that you found one."

She never had any return of this condition. Twenty years later, she wrote a letter confirming these facts.

As the sick came to our door, we had to make our decision; were we to lead the normal lives of young married people—or to dedicate ourselves and our free time to this work? As more and more came, the problem grew more immediate. In our hearts we had already made it. But we still had to face up to what was happening. One night, after a long evening, Olga said, "We cannot turn from them, can we?"

I answered, "No. We cannot. And will not."

That was all. We both understood what it meant.

On one occasion an executive employed at the Glenn L. Martin Company had a tonsillectomy. This operation had been suggested by his physician as a way of curing a bad case of hives that would not respond to regular treatment. Not only did the operation result in a serious hemorrhaging that almost cost his life, the hives failed to improve. They grew larger and more agonizing.

One day this man, during a meeting at the plant, described all that he had been and still was going through. Listening to his story, several of the men asked him why he didn't try me—I happened to be present at the meeting. "Why don't you let Ambrose treat you?" the men suggested.

The man laughed and said, "How much will you cost me for a treatment, Ambrose? Fifty or a hundred a visit?"

I said, "It never 'costs' anyone anything."

He laughed again, and the others began to tell him that he ought to take this suggestion seriously because I did have a reputation as a channel for healing.

"Well, all right—maybe I will," he said. "I can't see what harm it can do. These things can't get any worse. Most of the time I'm going mad with them. I'll try anything at this point."

The following night he came to our home and up to the healing room where I administered healing. He was in serious pain and agonizing itching. He had lost twenty-five pounds since the operation.

And he still had hives at his joints. I administered spiritual healing that night. By the time it was over—the healing session lasted approximately ten minutes—he informed me that the pain was gone. The hives were still quite visible but pain and itching had disappeared.

Within the space of ensuing weekly treatments all the hives were gone—permanently. And all the pain.

During his second visit for treatment an interesting psychic episode occurred. That night there were about eighteen persons in the living room downstairs, including the hive-ridden executive from our plant. Olga was with them, helping to put them at ease. Some of those present were there with children.

It was a pleasant gathering, there was nothing grim or fore-boding about it. One of the men suggested that Olga read their palms. Of course she knew nothing of the subject but it was suggested all in the spirit of fun and nothing more. Olga did know something about each one and so, although her palmistry was probably very poor, her character reading was good.

When she came to our special patient, however, she was a little nervous; he was, after all, one of the executives of the company in which her husband worked. However, when she reached him, as she explained it later, she became clairvoyant when she took his hand in hers, she saw, standing at his side, the man's mother. This spirit told her things that had happened to her in Germany, how she passed away, and the warm relationship she had known with her son. She also related a story of how he had fallen out of a tree as a boy, suffering an injury to his leg which had caused him pain in some measure ever since. She mentioned and named his Aunt Lily in California, with whom he had lived for a time, and she went into other details of his personal life.

No one in the room knew a thing about his personal background or history. But as Olga related to him all of these facts that the spirit of the mother had told her, the man suddenly burst into tears. "That is my beloved mother," he told the group.

Because of the Nazis, he told them, he was not permitted to go into Germany during his mother's last illness, a fact which had caused him much suffering. The revelations of his mother that night changed his whole outlook and philosophy and had a pro-found effect on his life. For he was not a believer, but rather an agnostic, a scientist who did not give his belief easily.

One additional story belongs in this highlighting of early cases. It concerns Olga herself.

Some time before our marriage Olga had injured her left hand in a fall on an icy sidewalk. Following this mishap a small lump appeared in the injured area. It did not disappear, but grew larger until it was as big as a good-sized walnut.

Olga had been praying, unknown to me, that this lump would disappear. She was a little alarmed at the size of it, the fact that it did not grow smaller and that it was causing her considerable pain. Several of our doctor friends had tried their skills on it, without success. Several recommended surgery, with the warning that because of the position of the lump, it could cause loss of the use of the hand.

I had noticed it and wondered about it but my intuition said let Olga speak of it, if she wanted me to help her. There are times when gifted persons are not able to help themselves, even though they can help others.

At last one night the pain in her wrist and hand became almost unbearable. She had endured this for some time without mentioning it to me; now it had reached the breaking point. Lying in bed, in the dark, with tears in her eyes from this pain, she prayed to God to give her some direction. The next instant, Olga disclosed later, she was hearing words spoken in a voice that seemed quite real and distinct: "Ask Ambrose to touch your wrist."

At that moment all that I knew, lying in bed beside my wife, was that she turned and said to me, "Dear, will you please touch my wrist and heal it?"

Half asleep, I heard her words. I said, "I have been wondering when you were going to ask me."

Then I reached out and held her hand and her wrist at the point just above the hand itself where the lump had formed. I held it, I think, only a few seconds, perhaps ten or fifteen. Something told me this was all that I needed to do.

I let go her wrist and went to sleep.

We did not mention this incident in the morning, nor look at or speak of the lump on her wrist. Because of its unusual significance Olga later set down her record of that event.

"That morning I was in a hurry to get breakfast for Ambrose who was a trifle late for work. I did not think about my wrist or hand at all. After breakfast I went out with Ambrose to the garage.

He got into the car and drove off, and I closed the garage doors and started back to the house.

"A next-door neighbor was hanging out the morning wash, and I stopped a moment to chat with her. As we were talking she suddenly said, 'Oh, I see you've had that awful lump on your wrist removed.'

"I looked down at my hand and saw that the lump had disappeared.

"I have seen hundreds of healings and with Ambrose and in my own work have helped to bring healing to many individuals. But it is quite something else when it happens to you. I briefly commented on the lump being gone and hurried into the house.

"I sat down on a kitchen chair, quite overwhelmed. With tears in my eyes, I kept saying out loud, 'Thank you, thank you, dear God, thank you.'

"That night when Ambrose came home the first thing I did was to show him the wrist. I said, 'It's gone—it's gone.'

"Tears came into his eyes as he joined me in giving prayerful thanks to God for this healing."

That was many years ago. Neither the lump nor the pain returned.

11 &~ Healing Hands

All of our studies of Scripture bear out the fact that the Christian position not only accepts healing as part of its mission, but makes it a responsibility for those who have been given this particular gift. One of the clearest statements on this is found in I Corinthians 12:4-11.

"Now there are varieties of gifts, but the same Spirit; and there are varieties of service, but the same Lord; and there are varieties of working, but it is the same God who inspires them all in every one. To each is given the manifestation of the Spirit for the common good. To one is given through the Spirit the utterance of wisdom, and to another the utterance of knowledge according to the same Spirit, to another faith by the same Spirit, to another gifts of healing by the one Spirit, to another the working of miracles, to another prophecy, to another the ability to distinguish between spirits, to another various kinds of tongues, to another the interpretation of tongues. All these are inspired by one and the same Spirit, who apportions to each one individually as he wills."

It was in this sense of dedication that we had set upon this ministry. We knew that it would involve some sacrifice of time and energy which we would give willingly. In Cleveland Olga led a life of social interests, music, cultural activities of many kinds. These had always been an important part of her family life and background. She gave them up willingly.

The question of payment continued to haunt us. Many people simply would not believe that we not only did not accept but would not accept payment. We have been offered literally tens of thousands of dollars. We have been offered expensive gifts. One grateful woman offered to give us a large home. It was far more than we could ever hope to afford, it was a lovely new home and was indeed tempting. But we had to tell her "no." A wealthy woman from a Southern state handed us a signed check, made out to me, and signed by her, with no amount written in. "Make it for whatever figure you wish," this woman said.

I have no idea how large a figure was in her mind. It might have been thousands of dollars or tens of thousands. It did not matter for we could not accept it, whatever it was. Gently we explained our reasons. "We're grateful," Olga told her, "that my husband has a good position, and while we are not rich we are not in need of money. So this work we give freely. If we gave all our time to this, then I suppose we would have to charge something in order to live comfortably. That would be different."

We do not try to judge others. The standards that we set for ourselves are those that seem right for our work. But this is not to disparage those who through the force of other circumstances may be compelled to charge some payment to carry on this work. The issue is entirely personal. The laborer *is* worthy of his hire even in the field of spiritual healing, so long as he does not misuse the healing gift or distort its purpose for individual gain, or in any way seek to exploit human suffering for personal gain.

At the beginning we had to learn, to work our way forward. Much of it was inspiration; one learns the technique from the proper impression. One learns the value of study groups to examine the reports of the experiences of others. One learns to develop and use techniques and approaches best suited to the situation. For example, in absent treatment, where the patient is not known, I have found the use of a photograph of great value. It enables me to envision the individual. Visualization develops the second state: concentration of force in that direction, healing force. Often this can be accomplished in a moment or two. One must learn not to press further, to relax, to remove personal identity from the scene and let the full force work which has been directed toward the person through me.

In all things, of course, the energy of love itself—compassionate healing love—is a paramount factor. This is not mere words, sentimentality, pretty phrases; the chemistry of compassion is the most powerful factor in religion and most of all in religious healing. One must love, one must enfold one's patient in compassion, one must yearn for him or her to get well, to be whole, to be without suffering or pain. Without this driving force of compassionate love nothing whatsoever is likely to happen.

We began our ministry with children. We loved them for themselves and we loved them a little more than might ordinarily have been the case because our two children were taken from us. This love was very real with us and very strong.

To the youngsters who were brought to us or whom we went to see, we were always Uncle Ambrose and Aunt Olga. These were our names, and to the children we were very close and our relationship was very real. To them—and to us.

One infant girl who was brought to me had developed at the age of three months a cyst inside her mouth. This cyst grew to a point where it would extrude from the infant's mouth. The doctor insisted the cyst be removed by surgery. Before agreeing to this the parents brought the infant to our house. I held the little girl in my arms in the quiet of the healing room for perhaps as long as twenty minutes; then I handed the sleeping child to the mother.

In the morning the mother called to tell me that the cyst had disappeared overnight. When she took the infant to the physician, he did not know how to explain it but he agreed that need for the operation no longer existed.

An even more anomolous episode occurred when this infant girl was a little more than a year old. She had developed a bad case of the croup. The mother had taken her to the doctor; the medication had not proved helpful. One night the mother called me from the drugstore, about a ten-minute walk from where she lived, and asked me to please send her child spiritual healing. She had gone to the drugstore to get medicine prescribed by the doctor for the infant. She said she was afraid the child was going to choke to death because it was having great difficulty in getting its breath. I said to her, "You go home immediately, put the child on your lap, place your right hand over its chest and your left hand on its back." She said she would do this. I went back to the living room and sat down with some other persons who had come in to chat about some of their problems.

In the midst of the conversation I felt an overwhelming force taking hold of me, drawing on me. I found myself compelled to turn my whole body in the direction in which this woman and her family lived. I told the others present that I was being forced to do this. I said that I felt something being extruded out of my solar plexus, an invisible cylindrical substance perhaps eight inches in diameter. It seemed to me to be drawn toward the house where this woman lived.

This lasted only a moment. I described to the others what I was experiencing. I then felt a sense of calm, I forgot the incident, I turned back to our discussion.

The following morning the mother called. She said she had experienced a miracle the night before. She said she had done exactly what I had told her to do with the infant, taking the child up, holding her exactly as instructed. She said that in a few seconds the child coughed up a lot of mucus, relaxed and went to sleep. She said at the same time she felt a tremendous vibration going down her arms. This occurred at exactly the time that I experienced the pull and power of invisible energies in our living room.

The child woke up that morning, she said, completely free of croup.

What was the physical mechanism by which healing was achieved? What was the force I felt within me that turned me around in my chair?

As a scientist and a student I have studied the methods of

spiritual healing in tests of various kinds, but the fact is that none of the studies have yet disclosed the functional mechanism. It is entirely possible that we will never find the answer in terms of the physical. We are talking about techniques primarily metaphysical in character.

Olga was equally involved in many of these healings. Olga's psychic powers range in a wider area in many cases than mine; she receives impulses and impressions in a different way entirely. Her clairaudience (hearing of spirit voices) is more developed and more active. Often her gifts serve as a complement to mine, in that she will receive information or guidance which fills in impressions I receive by another avenue.

Olga received a call from a woman who had just been told that her grown daughter, who lived in Grosse Point, Michigan, had developed a lump on her neck the size of a doorknob. The mother was fearful that it might be a dangerous malignancy. Olga instead told the woman over the phone, "No, it is not malignant at all. I know what is wrong."

Psychically the information had come to her instantaneously. "This lump is caused by dead white corpuscles," she stated.

"That's an extraordinary thing to say in view of the circumstances," the mother said.

She then explained that before the growth had appeared the doctor had been giving the girl treatments of a new type: He had been injecting her with scraping from her tonsils. The physician had developed a large clinetele for this technique which he claimed would reduce body infections of many kinds.

Olga had known nothing about this. But it was apparent that the technique was not working with the daughter. She suggested that the mother instruct the daughter to see another doctor immediately, perhaps two, and get further diagnostic opinion.

The mother said she would call Grosse Point as soon as she hung up.

The woman went to another physician who was uncertain about the case and said that the lump might be a misplaced goiter. A third physician was able to state with complete certainty: "I have seen this kind of thing before and it is a collection of dead white corpuscles. Apparently they were being injected into your body for immunization."

There was no serious problem. All she had to do, he stated, was to stop taking these injections. The lump in the neck would subside in about six months.

That was precisely what happened.

Olga brings to spiritual healing a remarkable exuberance that many people do not understand. Olga does not accept the long drawn countenance—or even the long-drawn multisyllabic words —as the essential aura in which all things spiritual must be surrounded. But underlying her seeming lightness is a depth of understanding at its purest level and simplicity. Olga reaches out with the ingenuous delight and cosmic acceptance of a child at play.

I remember long ago an incident at our home on Belair Road in Baltimore, which was to be of tremendous importance in our own lives, although when it began one might not have thought so. It involves a spirit who has appeared to us many times. He is an Indian. We know little about his background except that he is seven feet tall and his name is XYZ. He says that is enough for us to know.

A strange warmth fills the room when this spirit is present, a force of permeating and selfless love, an emanation of good.

One morning in the early fall of 1941, while Olga was clearing up the breakfast dishes in the kitchen sink, XYZ decided to pay a visit. Olga heard him say, "It is time for you to move."

As neither Olga nor I had even discussed the possibility of moving, this was a startling suggestion, from whatever realm. But Olga said only, "And just where are we supposed to move? And what will Ambrose say when I tell him?"

"He will exclaim, 'What? And what will you do with this house?'" XYZ answered.

"And where shall I look for houses?" Olga asked.

XYZ answered that she was to look in the telephone directory for a real estate firm with the name Roland Park.

Olga had never heard of such a firm before, but she looked and there it was—Roland Park Real Estate brokers. Beguiled by this adventure, she called the number and told the man she was interested in seeing houses. The rest of the day she spent being driven all over Baltimore. At each house, however, Olga would hear clairaudiently, "It is not for you . . ."

Olga explained to the real estate man that the houses shown were not suitable to our needs.

The real estate man began to grow very discouraged. I think he would have been more so if he had known the true situation. He finally informed my wife that she had seen virtually every vacant house in the city, and he had nothing left to show her unless she cared to look at some unfinished places going up in the Northwood Section.

Northwood was, and remains, a charming section of Baltimore. But the house was not only unfinished at that stage, it was little more than a foundation and a few struts. Yet Olga heard the unheard words: *"This is your house . . . you must put down a plank . . . go on in . . ."*

The plank was put down and Olga walked into the floorless structure of a house that was, itself, at that moment little more than a spirit and a vision But to Olga it was all there before her.

Up the street there was a house of very similar design, furnished and already sold, and this we were able to enter to see what the house would be like. There was no doubt in Olga's mind. XYZ had found the dream house she had wanted all her life.

To be candid, she did not reveal all of this to me when I arrived home. Her feminine intuitions are not unlike that of all women when they have seen something they think their husbands ought to buy.

When I arrived home from my day's toil, she greeted me in the most casual way with the information that she had been out for the afternoon. Nothing wrong with that. Until she added that she had been out looking for a new house. She then began to talk about the dream house in Northwood. She was trying to explain what had led her to do all this, but I was too angry even to listen. "What?" I cried out. "And what will you do with this house? What are we going to use for money?"

Then, exactly like all other husbands, I suppose, I simmered down, and Olga began to tell me this incredible story.

Only to me, as to Olga, XYZ was a friend from the other side.

The next morning I awakened about 5:00 A.M. I lay motionless, aware of forces around me, pressing in upon me. There was no doubt in my mind about what they were telling me. It was a kind of silent report. We were to move. We had to move . . .

I awakened Olga and told her. I said, "Look, I have to get to work early, but if you'll get up right away we could rush over and see that place you were telling me about before I go to work."

We got dressed hurriedly, ate a quick breakfast, and drove over to look at the framework of this house Olga had seen through the insistence of XYZ. By a good omen the contractor happened also to be there early that morning, waiting to receive a new shipment of lumber. He took us through the completed model house as well as the unfinished structure that would be ours. This is the house in which we write these words—we have lived here now more than a quarter century.

Before we left that morning, I had written and handed to the contractor a fifty-dollar check as a deposit to hold the house for us.

Olga has been and is especially good at what I call psychic diagnosis. She receives impressions which tell a problem. In one case she saw clairvoyantly a man's enlarged heart; she told me this and we talked with relatives of the man. He had a serious heart condition that Olga was certain had been wrongly diagnosed. She urgently suggested that X-rays be taken of the heart. This proved that Olga's diagnosis was correct.

Often she will see only the part of the body affected, and she will see exactly what is wrong. She is equally able to obtain healing impressions with children. And also with animals. Indeed her healing of animals is a kind of specialty; she has a deep love for them and they for her. At one time we had a whole casebook of animal healing.

A woman called to ask Olga's help: Her prize-winning French poodle had become paralyzed in his two hind legs. The veterinarian declared that the dog would have to be destroyed; he couldn't help him. Olga saw the dog psychically as she spoke with the woman on the telephone; she saw the dog's stomach filled with objects—twigs, stones, pebbles, and an assortment of other items he had swallowed. She told the woman this and suggested, "Have them pump out his stomach."

The woman at first insisted this couldn't be correct and refused to assent. But at last, realizing that she had no alternative, she agreed to carry out Olga's suggestion of getting the stomach pumped if the veterinarian felt it would be possible to do so safely. The "vet" consented to the process but said it was all nonsense and could be of no help.

The forced regurgitation brought up pebbles, stones, twigs, and all the other items Olga had seen clairvoyantly. Once the dog got this small geological collection out of his system, he was completely well.

Cats, dogs, horses, birds—even flowers—have all been responsive to Olga's healing prayers.

Once, in a flower show competition, Olga was invited to show cockscombs. The day before the show they were about one inch too small to win any prizes. I remember seeing her look at them and say, I suppose more as an urgent wish than anything else, "Please grow an inch for the show tomorrow."

The following day at the show they were, by measurement, one and a half inches taller than the day before and won a blue ribbon.

These are the incidents of our lives that we live with the often seemingly small moments and experiences; yet, like the larger and more dramatic incidents, they represent integral components of our story.

And one of these surely was Caesar, a boxer.

He lived next door. He was one of those big, slow, easy dogs who kept to himself, but everyone on the block knew him.

Caesar was growing old and one day he didn't respond to his owner's calls. A checkup disclosed that the dog was deaf. It was a sad thing—the silent world of Caesar.

Some weeks after this development the dog came over to our yard to visit with Olga. This was unusual for Caesar. He came up to Olga, looked at her and deliberately put his head against Olga, rubbing his ears against her, almost asking her help. This was *not* usual.

Olga touched the dog's head, held his ears in her hand for some seconds. The following morning Caesar was back again, standing there expectantly. This in a dog that previously wouldn't let any-one touch his head because of the trauma suffered when his ears were altered. Well—here he was for a second treatment! So Olga gave him one, with all the love she has for these animals.

The next day Caesar's owner stopped by. She asked Olga in a curious tone, "Did you do something to my dog?"

Olga said, "Why?"

"I saw you touch his ears and head yesterday morning. Today he can hear perfectly. He appears to be completely cured of his deafness."

And indeed he was!

One young couple who knew of our work called in great distress about a cat. The cat had been badly mauled and was close to death. They knew of Olga's special interest in all animals. Could she help a cat, that was in pain and close to death?

Let me quote the letter these two people wrote to us at a later time:

Dear Olga and Ambrose:

Watching our lovely cat, which we call "Good Girl," stretching happily in the sun the other day, Dick and I found it hard to realize that only a few months ago, she had crawled home, literally crushed, having been attacked by two Dalmatians in a neighbor's yard. Her sides were completely caved in and we found a large tooth wound in her stomach. Her breathing was fast and shallow and she collapsed after crawling to a far corner under our daughter's bed. We could not move her as she was evidently bleeding internally, and she could not take milk, not having the strength to move her tongue. We decided the last kindness we could show her was to have her put to sleep. We were all deeply distressed, and our youngest daughter, Sue, begged us to call you and Ambrose for help.

We hesitated to do this, all of us having received so much of your time and help for the past several years, the most priceless of all, the beautiful spiritual life to which you have led us, and a glorious happiness we never dreamed possible.

Sue's helpless grief decided me. I called for help for "Good Girl" and "our Olga" came to the front for us, as in our hearts we knew you would. Your calm assurance that Good Girl would fully recover left no room for doubt in our minds. One hour after you told me you would hold healing prayers for kitty she took her first bottle of milk and water. Three days later she was moving around the house—within two weeks her ribs had healed as well as the wound in her stomach.

God has been so good to us, can hardly find words to express our gratitude. But kitty especially wants to thank you for her tenth life.

Affectionately,
(Signed) Dot and Dick Coleman

12 &ᴥ The New Life Clinic

The clinic was more than merely a clinic for those who wanted to try something new, more than a mere innovation. There were other clinics, and other religious healing going on in all faiths. The New Life Clinic was a blend of faith and practicality, bringing the injunction of Christ to His followers—to go forth and heal the sick—into a realistic, daily endeavor.

It began for Olga—for us—in January, 1950, with another of those series of coincidences that really could hardly be coincidences at all.

Olga was visiting a sister in New York City, while I was away on a business trip. A friend from Baltimore, whom Olga met in New York, told her that she had just read a newspaper article about a minister in Baltimore who had become interested in religious healing. His first healing service was to take place in his Baltimore church on Tuesday the following week. Since Olga and I were in this work, her friend was sure we would want to attend this meeting. But I was not due back in town until Wednesday and Olga had planned to stay until Wednesday in New York with her sister. However, on Monday morning at 6:00 A.M. Olga received a strong impression. It concerned not the healing service but my travel plans: *I was to be back sooner than expected; she should leave for home at once.*

My schedule had, in fact, changed, although I was unaware of it until one half hour before we left for Baltimore on the company plane. I was coming back late Tuesday rather than on Wednesday.

Acting on the goading psychic impressment, Olga arrived home in time to attend that healing service on Tuesday morning at the Mt. Vernon Place Methodist Church in Baltimore. As she came into the church, she met a lady we have both known many years, and they sat together. After the service this friend suggested that Olga should come up and meet the minister, Dr. Albert E. Day.

After the introduction they talked briefly. In a hurried sentence or two Olga managed to tell him of her own interest in healing. Dr. Day suggested that she stop in at his office and leave her name and address with his secretary. This Olga did—and promptly forgot about it, with no anticipation that she would ever hear from him again.

A series of happenings in our home on Thursday morning changed her entire thinking on this matter. I believe it best here to let Olga report this as she herself wrote it down, some time afterward, for our records:

". . . The following Thursday morning, around 8:00 A.M., I found my thoughts dwelling on the minister and the healing service. I made every effort to dismiss these thoughts; after all, the minister did not call me, so why all the excitement? However, by 8:30 that morning something that refused to be silenced insisted that the minister had need of my help and experience in the field of healing and that I was to phone him. I actually felt a strong push in the back that made me fall across the bed as I was making up the bed.

"I called out, 'O God, please don't let me make a fool of myself. I have never forced myself on anyone. The man has my phone number and if he is interested he will phone.' This was ridiculous —all the years my husband and I have been doing this work we have never gone to anyone offering our services. However, this command to contact the minister kept after me until at 9:00 A.M. I found myself calling the church office. The secretary informed me that Dr. Day was not in, was not expected because this was his day away from his office.

"I thanked the secretary with much relief; now I would not

make a fool of myself. Before I could hang up a voice said, 'I'm the associate minister—may I help?' Very briefly, I told him my name and my interest in healing. Dr. Day's associate minister said, 'Oh—we've been looking for your phone number—the secretary misplaced it. May I call at your home and see you?' I answered that I would rather see him at the church office. By 10:00 A.M., I was at the church office, wondering all the while what on earth possessed me to be doing all this.

"I explained to this young associate minister what my husband and I had been doing in the field of spiritual healing without benefit of any organization or group affiliations. In the midst of this conversation, the door of the office opened and in walked the minister himself, Dr. Day, much to the surprise of the associate minister who said, 'Why—what are you doing in here today?'

"Dr. Day then stated that he had suddenly felt that there was a compelling reason for him to come to his office even though this was his day to stay at home. Further discussion brought out my own experience of the morning, when I had felt this force within me urging me to phone the church. Dr. Day then asked me what time that was, and I said approximately eight thirty that morning. He seemed amazed, and told me that at precisely that time he was on his knees at his home in prayer, asking God to send him someone who knew something about the healing ministry to help in this new venture he was starting."

Olga was about to begin a new phase of her life in which I was to participate, too, in many ways: the beginning of a church-operated clinic which would reach out to literally thousands of persons seeking help, seeking healing, the New Life Clinic of this church in the heart of Baltimore, surrounded, indeed, by the buildings and classrooms and laboratories and operating rooms of one of the greatest hospitals and medical schools in the world, Johns Hopkins.

The Collect used in the Protestant Episcopal service of Holy Communion is the opening prayer of the New Life Clinic. To me it carries the force and meaning and attitude which Dr. Day and Olga brought to the service:

"Almighty God, unto whom all hearts are open, all desires known, and from whom no secrets are hid; Cleanse the thoughts of our hearts by the inspiration of thy Holy Spirit, that we may perfectly love thee, and worthily magnify thy holy Name; through Christ our Lord. Amen."

Today the wide interest in church healing services is found in virtually every major Protestant faith in America, particularly Presbyterian, Lutheran, Methodist, Episcopalian. The Mt. Vernon Place New Life Clinic, and others like it, recorded as the fore-runners and trail blazers in this work, reawakened the interest and attention of many other disciplines, physicians, nurses, psychiatrists, and psychologists. Today, as never before in modern history, many in these fields have begun to work together to understand and move forward in the quest of greater understanding. It is a quest for healing of the total individual—physically, mentally, emotionally, spiritually.

This was the goal that the clinic established with Dr. Day at the Mt. Vernon Place Methodist Church. I agreed to help in any way I could, to consult with Olga, Dr. Day, and others at the church. In addition Olga and I continued to work together at home on many of the clinic's cases.

To avoid any hint of commercialization, there was never a collection taken, nor a "love offering," nor gifts given or received by this clinic or its staff.

In the nine years in which this clinic was to remain in operation at Mt. Vernon Place Methodist Church, under the direction of Dr. Day and Olga Worrall, it was to become one of the most significant American healing centers to which people came from every section of the nation. (The New Life Clinic was to be moved, some years later, to the Mt. Washington Methodist Church in Baltimore, with the full co-operation of the Rev. Robert G. Kirkley, a firm believer in spiritual healing.)

The numbers coming to the clinic, of course, grew steadily over the years. The sessions remained simple, the techniques quite direct and uncomplicated. We talked with those who came to see Dr. Day or myself, counseled with them; Olga would discuss with them their problems, would explain the principles on which the clinic operated, the fact that it worked with and not against medical doctors and practice, that the individual had sought all the aid possible from medicine.

Wednesday morning at ten o'clock the session would begin with a half hour of teaching by Olga, followed by a half hour of quiet time in which those seeking healing or help would practice the techniques of meditation and contemplation and seek to bring themselves into readiness to receive spiritual power and help. At eleven would come the healing service and the ministry of the laying on of hands.

It was in the spirit of quiet surrender to God, in this hush of certitude of His power, that the services were conducted.

They were held in a small chapel inside the main part of the church building. Eventually, as the numbers of those who attended increased, an additional room next to the chapel was also used. There were as many as a hundred or more at these weekly healing gatherings.

The response to this clinic was startling to many in the church. Olga and I had long since learned how quickly the word spreads, how hungry the world is for this kind of healing, how people reach out to something they can believe, something obviously not for profit or personal aggrandizement, not sham but truly healing.

Letters with requests for help began to pour into the clinic and to us personally at our home. Sometimes the individual patient would write; sometimes it would be a relative or a friend. All of those seeking healing were remembered in prayer at the services in the church, or each evening at nine when Olga and I held the quiet time of prayer and healing. We sent out letters, explaining the meaning of the nine o'clock period and asking all seeking help to join us at that time.

We also explained to those living in other time zones that it would be best to hold their period at a time coinciding with nine o'clock in Baltimore. But in the case of those in Europe, when they might have to sit up at two o'clock in the morning, we explained that they could pray at nine o'clock their time. Later, while they slept, when it was nine o'clock our time, we would pray for them, and join in their earlier prayer. In prayer, neither time nor space presents formidable barriers.

Each person who came seeking aid was interviewed by Dr. Day or Olga and his problem discussed. Olga often saw clairvoyantly what was the matter and would tell him so. Sometimes Dr. Day would come to her with special cases and she would deal with them.

A child of four years was brought by his parents. He was badly, grotesquely, cross-eyed. Physicians had told the parents that the eyes would have to be corrected surgically if the boy was ever to go to school. Before he was to have his operation, his mother wanted to ask at the clinic if they could help with spiritual therapy.

This was one of the clinic's very early cases; it was particularly important because of Olga's compassion for children, her compassion for this youngster whose eyes rolled uncontrolled in every direction.

The New Life Clinic service, as designed by Dr. Day and Olga, was extremely simple: a prayer, a hymn, a simple statement on some phase of affirmation of Divine power and glory, usually delivered by Dr. Day, sometimes by Olga—and this statement followed by the actual service and the laying on of hands at the altar.

In the healing period itself both Dr. Day and Olga worked at the same time at the altar, each with a single individual so that there were no more than two seeking healing before the altar at any given time.

The day that the cross-eyed boy came his parents helped him to the altar. The youngster knelt calmly and quietly. Olga put her hands on him and closed her eyes in a prayer to God.

As Olga explained it, "I asked God to heal his eyes. I held in my mind the image of his eyes being healed, well, completely well. I held in my mind the vision of Christ touching the boy's eyes and healing them."

From that day on a change started; the boy began to get better.

In three months after he began coming to these weekly sessions, his eyes were completely normal. He was able to enter school and four years later, according to the latest available information Olga had, he was going to classes, participating in all school activities— and did not even wear glasses.

The flow of cases continued. With a small volunteer staff, maintaining records became increasingly difficult. Often we would not learn about results until the individual wrote us.

I recall the case of Mrs. Fred Muehlberger who suffered from a complete loss of equilibrium. Two people had to help her to the altar the first time she came into the church. She was pale, gaunt, shadowed with the wearying darkness of fear and despair and sickness itself.

She too continued to come to services. In two weeks, she walked out—unhelped by anyone. In a month she was well and out shopping. She wrote to us at the clinic in April of that first year of the clinic's operations:

May I tell you at this time just how much God has done for me since that wonderful day when . . . I first heard of your New Life Clinic?

I had been in the hospital for the third time in less than five months with something terribly wrong with my head. I had lost my equilibrium. Each time I had to be taken to the hospital in an ambulance. The best doctors had been consulted, X-rays had been taken, and practically every test had been taken including an electro-encephalogram which indicated a brain tumor. Next came the horrible air injection to the brain—which ruled out the brain tumor. I was thankful that there wasn't a brain tumor, yet I was becoming despondent because no one knew what was wrong. I had resigned myself to believe God didn't want me to get well. . . .

A friend . . . told me of your New Life Clinic and the following Wednesday I was brought in to the chapel. Several days later, Reverend Fiscus* called at my home and talked with me and I told him of the terrible fear that had taken possession of me. He told me that this fear must be removed from my heart in order for God's love and healing to come in and he prayed with me. Almost immediately the fear began to go.

I have attended services at the clinic every Wednesday and Mr. Worrall has used his wonderful God-given power on me. I now enjoy a peace that I have never known before. . . .

I have seen my doctor after an absence of about eight weeks, and he is very pleased at the great improvement in me. I told him that I have been receiving the healing power of God through the New Life Clinic. He was very interested and after I finished telling him about it, his only prescription was to continue as I have been doing.

Thank you Dr. Day, Rev. Fiscus, Mrs. Worrall and Mr. Worrall for the good things you are doing. . . .

With hundreds of individuals coming to the Wednesday services, or writing and asking to be remembered in prayers by Olga and myself, as well as by Dr. Day at the weekly services, many healings resulted, too many indeed even to begin to describe all of them. They covered every range of illness. Many must have been what doctors now call psychosomatic illness, where the symptoms, while real, have psychological origin. Many were functional illnesses that also could have some real psychological base. Many were what is called organic, strictly physical, so proven and diagnosed by X-rays, blood tests, and other records. Healings occurred right at the altar in some instances, during the administration of the laying on of hands, and prayer.

A woman came to the clinic to pray one morning, the day before she was to be operated on for removal of a growth on her

* One of the assistants in the church.

eye. When she arrived at the doctor's office the following day, the physician with great amazement informed her that the growth that was to have required serious eye surgery had become so loose he was able to lift it off with a pair of tweezers.

A brain tumor operation was called off by a surgeon only a few hours before it was to have taken place because tests indicated the tumor had disappeared. The man involved had been "preparing" himself for this operation by attending sessions of the clinic and coming to the church regularly for prayer.

A case of considerable importance involved a high official of one of the major league ball clubs who had a growth on his throat which had been diagnosed as cancerous. When he came to the altar for healing, Olga placed her hands on his neck, her left hand on the front part of his throat, the right hand on the back. She held her fingers in this position for a few moments, and felt what she described later as a tingling sensation go through her hands. At the same moment, the man himself looked up and said, "I feel terrific heat going into my throat."

The following Wednesday the baseball executive returned and asked Olga if she would place her hands on his neck again as she had done the previous week, because his throat felt so much better and he believed further therapy of this nature was indicated. He said also that he had an appointment after the service with a cancer specialist.

Olga placed her hands again on his throat as she had at the previous session and again the man experienced intense heat passing from her fingers into his throat. (This heat had nothing to do with actual physical pressure.) Olga's fingers were not exerting any pressure but were held lightly against the skin.

That night there was an evening service at the church. Dr. Day was in his office just prior to this service when a man barged into the office, thoroughly distraught. It was the cancer specialist. He demanded of Dr. Day, "What have you done with my patient?"

Dr. Day was frightened. He did not know what had happened. Further, the Johns Hopkins specialist was a member of the board of the Mt. Vernon Place Methodist Church. He then proceeded to tell Dr. Day that the patient had come to him following a session of the New Life Clinic and that the cancer which had been the size of a half dollar was gone and all that remained was a scar about as thin as a thread.

The growth did not return. The baseball man at the last report we had was retired and living happily in Florida.

Although the clinic staff tried to pre-interview everyone who came seeking healing before they actually went to the altar during the Wednesday service, there were instances where strangers arrived that no one had seen or talked with previously.

One day a white-haired woman attired in a navy blue dress came and knelt at the altar before Olga. Olga had not seen her before and asked the aged woman gently, "What do you want me to pray for especially?"

The woman looked up and said, "I don't know!"

She bowed her head. At that very moment Olga perceived a man at her side, a spirit. This spirit informed Olga, "I am her husband. I died last week. Tell her I am still with her and not to mourn for me."

Psychic episodes certainly were not new to Olga. But this was a church service and many persons were looking on. And many of them, including the woman herself, might not understand such a thing as this. Olga was not sure at first what to say. She decided after an instant to tell the woman. She leaned close to the woman, whispering to her exactly what she had seen and repeating the words that had come to her from the spirit of the man. The woman cried out, "My God! My God! I have been praying to God for some proof of my husband's survival. He died last week."

Several weeks later this woman returned to the clinic to tell Olga, "My child, you have made an old woman happy. I can carry on now. I know—I no longer hope but I know—my husband lives, he is with me."

13 ❧ Case History

Many requests for healing at the New Life Clinic came to us through ministers of other churches. A Methodist minister, Dr. Harold McClay of Baltimore and Cumberland, brought us a man who had suffered severe injury to his eyes in an accident involving an acetylene torch. The physician told him he would have to learn braille as he had lost virtually all vision and could not regain it. The man came regularly to our sessions; Olga gave him healing through the laying on of hands; we held him in our thoughts during the nine o'clock prayer hour which Olga and I continued in the evenings at our home. This man began to gain his vision again, in the lower section of the eye. Gradually, this strengthened to a point where he could see.

Another case involved a Presbyterian minister, Dr. Hugh F. Craven. His son, a medical doctor, who often attended the New Life Clinic, came to see me and asked if I would try to reach his father, ill with a heart ailment, by absent healing. The minister was told by his son that I would be holding him in healing prayer each night at nine o'clock and Olga would be praying for him at the church service.

Several weeks later the minister wrote to his son that he had followed the absent healing instructions and that he was getting better. The pains had begun to diminish; his whole condition was improved; he was far more able to carry on his active and demanding labors for his church.

Three months later he wrote again to say that he was infinitely better, his whole condition had improved; he no longer had pain, no longer felt weak or worn out at the end of a day. He continued:

Many times a day I thank God for what He has done for me and can do for my many friends . . .

The one regret I have is that I did not know or believe that the healing power of God could be had for the body, as the soul can be forgiven and made to rejoice again. If I had only known it, how much help I could have given men and women, through Christ Jesus. Yet God has been trying to tell me this great fact for years; yet I have been afraid. I am planning on attending some of your spiritual healing meetings or services that I may know more. . . .

A few minutes before one healing service at the Mt. Washington Methodist Church was to begin, a woman approached Olga to ask if special prayers could be said for her husband who was quite ill. She said her name was Mrs. Clarence Snyder. She told that the doctor was unable to find out just what was the matter with the husband.

Olga listened to the woman and, as she so frequently does, she was also listening to the spiritual guidance or intuition if one wishes to call it that. In a moment Olga knew what was the matter. She informed the woman that her husband had a congested gall bladder, a spastic gall duct, and that through proper medication, diet, and prayer, the condition would correct itself. A week later, according to Olga's notes on the case, the woman returned to the clinic in a state of deep concern. Her husband was no better; in fact, after being examined by several doctors, the diagnosis and X-rays confirmed cancer of the pancreas. An operation was to be performed and the woman was told that her husband's life "wasn't worth a nickle." Olga insisted that the diagnosis was incorrect. The woman then asked Olga to speak to the doctor; this Olga refused to do, but she did agree to talk to the doctor if he called her. The next day the doctor did indeed phone. Olga told him what her diagnosis was; the physician asked her who she was and then hung up. The man was operated on, and the surgeon discovered that the pancreas was healthy. Remembering Olga's remarks, the surgeon made a gall bladder incision and discovered that indeed the gall bladder was at fault; the organ was removed. The doctor rushed into the waiting room without first removing his gown to inform Mrs. Snyder that her husband did not have cancer and then remarked, "That woman is a terrific prayer, a large gall stone had split into three pieces and with the next gall bladder spasm it would have been ejected."

Shortly afterward Mrs. Snyder wrote:

My husband came home from the hospital much sooner than is normal for such an operation, two incisions had to heal. Several weeks later, my husband went back to the hospital for a checkup and all the doctors can't figure out how they could have made such a wrong diagnosis; they rechecked the X-rays and tests, and still can't figure out what happened.

I know that prayers healed my husband and that Mrs. Worrall knew what she was talking about. My husband is back at work and enjoying good health. The Heavenly Father surely heard our prayers.*

The number of stories arising out of cases at the clinic could be multiplied, the number of healings, of letters. To recount each would be repetitious and purposeless. Nor is there much to be gained, on the other side, by reporting those cases where healing did not occur. The clinic was a pattern, not only of success and failure, but also of human beings seeking alleviation of pain for themselves and others and reaching out, in their search, to God's healing.

Each case had its drama, its struggle of good against evil, health against sickness, wholeness against destruction, pain, death. And each case was its own victory; even in failure, some help was given, some peace of mind, some acceptance of the universe of love. At least this much.

Two cases I consider of extreme importance because of the circumstances and the individuals concerned.

One of these is clearly outlined in the firsthand words of a well-known physician, whose name must be withheld here to

---

* Text of entire letter appears in Appendix A.

protect his professional background. In a statement he made to a group of medical and clerical associates at the Order of St. Luke Seminar held in Baltimore, he said:

Gentlemen: I am a physician whose training and experience has been in the field of General Surgery, which speciality I practiced for three years. . . .

After five years of intensive and meticulous study in the area of "healing," it seems to me that there is "something here" which needs greater study and illumination. Let me give you an example: In 1956 or so, a nurse who was psychiatrically oriented, consulted me for the problem of abdominal lymphosarcomatosis. The diagnosis was made microscopically by men trained at Cancer Memorial in New York City. Therefore, we must consider the idea that the diagnosis was "probably" accurate. At any rate, the nurse believed the diagnosis and was given therapeutic dosages of X-ray therapy and that was followed with adequate amounts of nitrogen mustard therapy.

When we saw her, she had lost weight from about 140 to 106 or so; she had a tumor as large as your head in her abdomen—visible to the naked eye. She was getting 200 mgm of Demerol 3–4 times a day for severe pain and was "existing" on a liquid diet. The husband's mother and father cared for the 3 children, all girls, while they were under our care.

For a week, intensive, specified "spiritual therapy" was administered to the woman and her husband on a 3-hour per day basis. Following this, she was free of pain at the end of the week and was able to tolerate a semi-solid diet.

Acting upon "inner-guidance," the suggestion was made that she and her husband stop at a "healing service" held each Wednesday morning at which my friend, Mrs. Olga Worrall, participated.

The couple followed the advice. The woman felt guided to approach Mrs. Worrall, who without any type of suggestion was guided to "lay hands" upon the nurse's abdomen.

While no objective phenomena were noted, the nurse reported that she had "the sensation of a big corkscrew turning in my stomach." They went on their way back to New Jersey—the tumor still obviously present.

She gradually returned to her professional duties. Her visit occurred in May, as I remember, and by November the tumor was completely gone. She has returned for follow-up checks on several occasions and is completely well.

Since that time, she had undertaken additional college work, and greater professional responsibilities than she had ever faced before her illness.

The man who did her X-ray diagnostic work and therapy even approached her and asked that she submit to further X-ray diagnosis in an effort to determine what had occurred. She did, and he was unable to find any remains of pathology.

Gentlemen, I submit to you, *Something* happened here. If we are to demand homage and respect from the public-at-large in the role of guiding public and personal health policies, it is also our obligation, in my opinion, to make an honest and scientific effort to understand this phenomena and co-operate with it to the best of our ability.

Yet, to me, the most striking case in which Dr. Day, the clinic, Olga, and I were concerned was that which brought in Duke University's world-renowned Dr. J. B. Rhine, founder of Duke's special laboratory for parapsychological studies.

It began in 1951 when Dr. Day asked Olga if she and I could hold a friend of his in our prayers. The friend, he said, was Gerald Heard. Olga happened not to have heard of this important religious lecturer and philosopher. Nor had I. Dr. Day explained that Gerald Heard was very much involved in spiritual and religious movements. Dr. Day had just been with his friend and was very disturbed at how ill the man appeared to be. Heard had been scheduled to attend a seminar on prayer, but it was doubtful that he could keep his engagement because of his physcial condition.

Olga's notes, recorded upon her return home in the afternoon after this episode, are as follows:

"Just before we were to leave the study for the Chapel, Dr. Day requested that Ambrose and I hold his friend, Gerald Heard, in our healing prayers. He seemed deeply concerned over the health of his friend. Dr. Day told me that he promised his friend that if he would keep his speaking engagement for the coming Seminar we would take care of his health.

"I found myself listening with one ear to what Dr. Day was saying, and with the other ear, I was hearing what a woman dressed in white was telling me. I heard her say, 'I am Gerald's grandmother. He will recognize me by this diamond guard ring set with two diamonds.' She continued, 'I am the only one in the family who understood Gerald, and I continue my interest in his spiritual activities. Give him my love.' Dr. Day very hurriedly made a note of what I had received from this spirit who claimed to be Mr. Heard's grandmother. We then left for the chapel."

During our prayer period in our home that Wednesday evening Gerald Heard's grandmother again appeared to Olga.

She gave Olga the following message:

"My grandson's illness has been caused by a serious fall he suffered when a very small child. This has resulted in . . . causing the colon to be spastic, and one leg is shorter than the other. We are already sending him spiritual healing, using you and Ambrose as our channels."

The following day was Thanksgiving, and we attended the service at Mt. Vernon Place Methodist Church. After the service Olga told Dr. Day the information she had received the evening before from Gerald's grandmother. Dr. Day stated that he knew nothing of the things Olga received, but that he would make a note of this information and pass it on to Mr. Heard.

On the following Sunday evening, during our period of prayer and meditation, the grandmother again appeared to Olga. Olga shared the message with me as she was receiving it:

"The grandmother is . . . delighted she is to be able to inform her grandson, through us, of her help and concern for him. She says the healing is already being received by him and all will be well. She says her grandson wears a beard! She is fading away from my sight with the thought of deep gratitude for listening to her."

The next morning, Dr. Day was given this information.

Several years later, Mr. Gerald Heard was visiting Duke University and met with Dr. J. B. Rhine. Mr. Heard discussed with Dr. Rhine the message that he had received from his grandmother through Olga's clairvoyance. Apparently, Dr. Rhine was impressed perhaps because of Mr. Heard's integrity and position in the field of education, and as a writer of note and a lecturer. There began an exchange of letters.

In 1956, Dr. Day received a letter from Dr. Rhine, asking for complete information about this case. In his letter to Dr. Day, dated July 6, 1956, he stated that Heard had authorized him to inquire further into the part which Mrs. Worrall played "in this interesting chain of experiences. . . ."

Dr. Rhine stated that the account of the story interested him a great deal because of the study they were conducting at Duke into the hypothesis of spiritual survival. He requested Dr. Day to answer four questions:

1. Did Dr. Day consider it likely that Mrs. Worrall knew anything about Mr. Heard's family and background?

2. How did he happen to serve as a link in this series of events?

3. Had Dr. Day introduced Mr. Heard to Mrs. Worrall?

4. What did Dr. Day himself know about Mr. Heard's grandmother?

Dr. Day's reply to Professor Rhine declared in part:

She [Olga] had never met Mr. Heard and knew nothing about him at all. But . . . she reported to me, in substance, as follows:
". . . Ask Gerald, the next time you see him, several questions. (1) Was he ever injured at the junction of the spine and hip anatomy. They tell me that there lies most of his difficulty, and they are going to help to heal him. (2) Ask him if he is working on a manuscript that is only half completed. He seems to be concerned about it. Tell him not to worry for he will be able to complete it. (3) Ask him if he had a grandmother who was very close to him. I see her, holding up her hand with an old-fashioned guard ring on her finger, and smiling and sending her love. . . ."

A month later, I went back to the University to attend another meeting. On my way over to the building where he was lecturing on the Philosophy of Religion, he and I had an opportunity to fall behind the others and have a private conversation. I said to him, "Olga wants me to ask you three questions." I then repeated the questions. His answers were:

(1) That twice he had been injured by a fall at the spot indicated by Mrs. Worrall. . . .

(2) In answer to the second question, he replied that he had been working on the Life of Asoka, the Indian saint, and it was only half completed. I delivered the message and assurance that Olga had given me.

(3) When I asked about his grandmother, his face shone with a great light, and he said happily, "She is the best friend I ever had." With that the conversation ended, for we had reached the University Building.

I did not see him until ten months later. He bounded out of the place like a boy. I said to him, "Gerald, you act like a boy." He replied, "Albert, I have never been so well in my life. I seem to have inexhaustible energy. It all dates back to the time when you gave me that message. It is the first time in my life that I have ever felt that anyone on the other side cared for me." You would have to know something of his history to understand the poignancy of that remark.

This, in outline, is the story. . . .

Olga, herself, also received a letter in which Professor Rhine at Duke probed for further information:

Did she still have a record of the actual script obtained containing the message for Mr. Heard? Could he get a verbatim copy of this script?

To complete the record in the Gerald Heard case, Olga's letter to Dr. Rhine, dated July 10, 1956, stated her recollection of the facts:

With reference to the communication that came through me for Mr. Gerald Heard, I am pleased to furnish the following information.

1. The information was received clairvoyantly and clairaudiently; therefore there is no script.

2. The message and information were not recorded but were reviewed and their essence captured soon after the occurrence. The following pertinent disclosures are from my records.

(a) On the Wednesday morning immediately preceding Thanksgiving Day in the year 1951, Dr. Albert E. Day asked me to ask my husband to hold a healing thought for his dear friend Gerald Heard. At that moment I saw clairvoyantly a woman who said she was Gerald Heard's grandmother. She held up her hand and showed me a diamond guard ring set with two diamonds and said that she could be recognized by Gerald because of this ring.

(b) The name Gerald Heard held no significance for me. I was not acquainted with his life or work in any way; neither did Dr. Day reveal to me any information about this man beyond his name.

(c) That evening my husband and I held healing thoughts for Gerald Heard. At this time, I again saw clairvoyantly the woman who said that she was Gerald's grandmother. She provided the information that Gerald had suffered a serious fall in early childhood which caused a twist of the lower part of the spine, a shortening of one leg, and a spastic colon. She also said that she had been extremely fond of Gerald and shared his interest in spiritual research.

(d) On the following Sunday, we again held healing thoughts for Gerald and again his grandmother appeared to me clairvoyantly. She told me that Gerald was writing a manuscript with which he was having some difficulty but he was not to worry about it because she would help him complete it. She informed me that Gerald wore a beard and that healing contact had been made.

(e) I conveyed this information to Dr. Day for I knew of no way to contact Mr. Heard other than through Dr. Day.

I do not consider this demonstration of psychic powers to be extraordinary in my experience. . . .

There is an interesting postscript regarding the facts as they first unfolded to Olga in 1951, five years before Rhine began his research into the case.

Olga met Gerald Heard when he came to Baltimore some months after the psychic episodes. He informed her then that he was very much improved in health and that the facts about his grandmother, including the guard ring with two diamonds which she wore on her ring finger, were all accurate.

He told her that in 1946 he had had an X-ray which showed that his fourth lumbar vertebra had been crushed. As Heard had been run over in 1902, he was convinced that the injury dated from that accident; however, the physician who examined the X-ray stated that he was practically certain the injury dated back to an even earlier date. When Heard wrote his brother for information about this, the brother stated that his grandmother had told him that she feared his back had been injured in early life. But no details were provided beyond that.

After Olga's message from the grandmother, Heard again wrote the brother in England, asking for information about any fall he might have suffered. To his astonishment the brother replied that he personally could verify Olga's whole story. Gerald Heard had been dropped as an infant by a nurse. The grandmother and the brother knew of it, but no one else, and they had agreed not to let Gerald or the family ever know that he had had this accident. To the brother it was a sacred promise and he had kept it all these years.

One additional "coincidence" is not on file regarding this unusual matter.

Dr. Day informed us, in discussing the case, that when he had given Gerald Heard the message from his grandmother, as received by Olga, dates were compared and it became apparent that on the same Wednesday night when his grandmother appeared to Olga, Gerald Heard's doorbell had rung three times and each time, when he went to answer it, there was no one at the door.

14 ⮡ Frontiers of Healing

The healing room we have set up in our home we think of as being part of the frontiers of faith.

As I sit in this room and seek to "tune in" on the patient, power comes to me. It actually builds within me. I can feel its presence. I am able also to feel it flowing from me.

The reactions of persons on these healing frontiers can help or hinder in healing. I can work with honest skeptics, but if a person says, for example, "It's no use anyway—I know already that you can't help me," there is probably no use trying to help, for the individual has erected barriers to keep healing from occurring.

But it must also be said of these frontiers that I have not only read of, but experienced in our own circles, cases of persons who did not believe and yet who were healed.

In spiritual healing knowledge often seems to come instantly, without effort or even awareness of how it reaches us. When I was younger, I would see a small ball of light about the size of a pea. It was like the dancing ball in the old-fashioned "movie sing." This dancing light would go directly to the place where my hands should be placed. Olga saw this light many times when she was in the room with me while I worked with a patient. In recent years I do not see this light. I seem to know without knowing how I know exactly what to do.

Knowledge of what is wrong may come in the healing room with the patient sitting before me. Yet it may sometimes come to me when the patient (whom I may never have seen at all) is hundreds of miles away. This knowledge comes as inspiration as soon as I have directed my attention to this patient's need, wherever he may be. This is truly what is called "knowledge without experience," and it does approach the pure, instinctive level of awareness.

I will know that in a certain case healing will occur. Something within me provides me with the information and there is no doubt, no question. I am not asking—I am stating: It is the same with diagnosis—if I get the diagnosis I know that it is a fact. This is not because the patient is in front of me or because I know the patient. I may never have seen him or her; the individual may be halfway around the world.

My kind of clairvoyant diagnosis is entirely spontaneous. I have no control over it. A man came to me and asked me to recommend a surgeon. I asked why he needed one. It was not for him, he said, but for his wife. She had a large lump on her face. I told him not to worry, she did not need an operation. What she had was only a lymph node.

The husband looked stunned. "How can you know that it is only a lymph node?" he demanded. "You never saw her in your life."

I admitted this was true. I said I wouldn't know a lymph node if I saw one. "But the information," I said, "has come to me. I know it is correct. If you will bring your wife to our house, I will see what we can do for her."

This the man did. I told Olga only that the woman had a lump on her face. *I did not tell her I had diagnosed it as a lymph node.* But the moment Olga saw her she said, "Oh, that is a lymph node."

This was entirely independent of my diagnosis.

I don't know why I said it was this kind of growth—or why Olga said it. Neither of us had any real understanding of what it meant. Yet I knew—simply knew, as did Olga also in this case— that no operation was called for. After the wife had been in our home a little time, and was relaxed, I took the lump between my fingers. In fifteen minutes it began to soften and reduce in size. I told the woman, "It is going away. Forget about it."

In just about twenty-four hours it had entirely disappeared.

There is no real control of these forces on the frontiers, for once we have relaxed and opened the spiritual channels to a point of receptivity the forces themselves act upon us in various ways not within our command. I am not speaking of negative forces, of such discarnate beings that bring discord. I am speaking of the frontiers of healing, the frontiers of the kingdom that is also ours.

For on these frontiers there is an unpredictability, a spontaneous factor. It is a region of quiet yet intense excitement.

There are many instances of this in our case records, often hastily jotted down for our files by either Olga or myself, or stowed away with letters and other documents and reports.

What are the limits of power on these frontiers? How great or small is our control?

I do not believe that anyone knows.

I recall a night when Olga and I were visiting a friend at her home on Kent Island, Maryland. We were sitting on the second floor porch of this home, chatting, when suddenly I saw, interposed and silhouetted between the moon and myself, the form of a man. He appeared to be standing there before me, looking up at the clouds and the moon. Our hostess was next to me on the porch, Olga beyond her. The form of the man had his back toward me. I told the hostess what I was seeing. She asked me to describe the man, and I explained that he had his back toward me. She said, "My husband John used to love to stand right there and watch the moonlight, the clouds, and the water."

The next instant the form of John disappeared from my sight. I thought no more of it. But a few minutes later there again appeared before me this same man, but he was so low in height that it appeared he was kneeling on the floor between the hostess and myself, his head just about level with my eyes. He was looking intently at the woman. I said to her, "I see the man. He is now directly between us. I am looking at the back of his head."

Our friend said, "Describe his head."

This I did. I explained that he was bald, with hair on the sides and the back, but there was a dark spot on the back of his head which looked as if it might be a little splotch of hair.

She asked me to point out on my own head where this splotch of darkness was. When I did she said, "You are describing John's head. My husband had a wen on his head in exactly that place. There is only one photograph that shows this. I have kept it hidden because I do not like this picture. Since my husband died I have visited many important mediums across the country and I have sought one proof of my husband's existence—and that is some report about that wen on his head. I did not receive one hint of it from any of the mediums I went to see. I wanted this description. You have given it to me."

And yet on this same frontier one of the most difficult answers to grasp in spiritual healing is the answer so natural that it appears to have been foreordained. A dramatic example of this came in the form of a postcard from a woman we had never before heard of. She lived in North Carolina. The card reached us from the post office because she had used no address and because the post office considered it urgent enough to hunt up the address itself. The card reads:

Dear Mr. Worrall: Please pray for ———— ———— of Asheville. He has just been shot by my son. In hospital—bullet lodged in head. I know he can be restored. I know God uses men like you—oh—I thank you—I am at the hospital and don't know your address, but I believe you can get this—I need your help. Mrs. J. S.

We regarded this as an emergency. These were people in need of immediate prayer and we treated the case in this way—not only during the regular nine o'clock prayer time, but also during a special period we set aside. Two weeks later we received the following communication:

Dear Mr. and Mrs. Worrall: Thank you so much for your quick response in prayer in my urgent need. I wrote you to pray for a man who had been accidentally shot by my son in the head. Well, that man is out of the hospital now and recovering beautifully. We praise God who did the miracle and answered your prayers and ours. If he had died, and without his testimony my son could have been convicted of manslaughter or even murder. Oh, I am so thankful. Yours in Christ, Mrs. J. S.

The frontier is a place not only of the unpredictable, but often of the deeply and spiritually rewarding experience.

Out of the files of this work, here are notes on one of these experiences, involving a world-famed United States ambassador, as recalled by Olga:

"I received a telephone call from a man who said his name was Joseph Grew. (Former Ambassador to Japan, Joseph E. Grew.) He wanted my husband to call at his home to give healing to his wife. I told him that we did not go to the homes of patients, that the patients had to come to us. He replied it was impossible for his wife to come to our home. He told me he would have his chauffeur pick us up and that he and his wife would like to have us dine with them. I again informed him that we did not visit patients' homes. He asked if he could speak to my husband. So I gave him my husband's office telephone number.

"I then received a call back from my husband, telling me that Mrs. Grew spoke to him over the telephone and that he agreed to go to Mr. and Mrs. Grew's home. Mr. Grew's chauffeur called for us. We had dinner with the immediate family, the daughter and son-in-law of the Grews. Mrs. Grew was unable to join us since she had sprained her ankle.

"After dinner we went upstairs into Mrs. Grew's sitting room and my husband administered spiritual healing. The swelling in the ankle was tremendously reduced and the black-and-blue marks faded away within twenty minutes. We asked the Ambassador how he had learned about us. He informed us that he was going to take Mrs. Grew to England to a healer for another ailment (Ménière's disease—an ear malady), but the healer in England cabled back to Ambassador Grew and said: 'Don't come to England. You have a healer in Baltimore named Ambrose Worrall.' (We were not able to heal Mrs. Grew's ear; the nerves had been surgically cut. But Ambrose was able to alleviate the pain and discomfort and this relief lasted for some time.)

"Shortly after that, New Year's Day, 1955, we received a telephone call from Ambassador Grew at eight o'clock in the morning. He asked Ambrose to see him. He had been desperately ill with what the doctors described as a huge stone in the gall bladder. They had wanted to operate on him when he was in Japan; however, the war came about and he didn't want the operation performed in Japan. Now it had recurred and doctors claimed he had to submit to an operation. However, he informed them that he would see Ambrose Worrall first.

"At two o'clock that afternoon he came to Baltimore driven by his chauffeur. Ambrose administered spiritual healing in the healing room. Ambrose advised Ambassador Grew that he was to return to Washington as quickly as possible because he was going to be nauseated. He said he knew this psychically. Ambrose had, through spiritual healing, released the bile in the gall bladder and, of course, as it emptied, it would cause nausea. The Ambassador made it to Washington in time and that day and the next he was nauseated. After that experience, he felt better. Within two days, the Ambassador was feeling much better. The attack was over and as far as we know he has never had a recurrence."

Here is another report Olga wrote for our files—about her own father:

"I dreamed that I was in my parents' living room. A violent windstorm was raging outdoors. I could feel the house shake—then I heard a terrific crashing sound coming from the second floor. I ran up the stairs, calling, 'Apo-Apo!' (Hungarian for 'Papa.') As I reached the top of the stairs, I discovered my father's bedroom completely destroyed. Although I could not see my father, I could hear my father talking with others, for I heard their voices as well, coming from the attic area. Then the voices faded away, as I kept calling my father. I awakened with a start. The clock showed 4:00 A.M. I was shaking. Then I began to understand about my dream. At once I 'knew' that it was not just a dream but an actual experience, and that something must have happened at home to my father. I could not go back to sleep. At 5:00 A.M. the phone rang. It was long distance—my family in Cleveland telling me that 'Apo' had passed away in his sleep an hour before—at approximately 4:00 A.M.

"That night my niece Dolly, who lived next door to my parents' home in Cleveland, called us long distance. I told her of my dream, mentioning the terrific windstorm. She said, 'Aunt Olga, you didn't dream all this. Last night Cleveland was struck by the worst windstorm in the history of the weather bureau."

Although neither Olga nor I go into any trance states, Olga does have a special gift of speaking in languages she herself does not know. Talking with a man of Russian background, Olga obtained messages for him in old classical Russian no longer spoken. In another case she relayed messages in seventeenth-century French, and in modern French as well, during an evening with a woman of French background. In both instances Olga spoke the languages fluently, although she does not speak French and has forgotten her "school Russian."

Most startling to me were a series of experiments we held with a remarkable scientist, physician, and medical researcher involved with one of the major hospitals in Maryland.

In many of the tests with this man of Arabic background Olga both spoke and wrote in Arabic. These tests went on over a period of more than ten years. Some of the findings were published in a magazine devoted largely to metaphysical, scientific, and parapsychological investigations.

The report on these matters is best given, I believe, in a letter to Olga and me, describing some of these events, written by the doctor himself:

I thought you might like to add to your records my personal experiences bordering on the metaphysical realm through the gift of clairvoyance that you both possess and which you have consecrated for the service of humanity. . . .

To eliminate any possible psychological influence or otherwise, I started with writing questions in Arabic, giving them to Olga to psychometrize. These questions referred to experiments, the results of some of which were unknown to me at the time. In this way, the subjective influences of the sensitive as well as the possibility of mind reading, were eliminated. This technique was repeated many times and in the majority of cases my questions were answered in a relevant way. Some of these answers have to do with strictly scientific and medical material pertaining to my research about which you knew nothing.

Allow me to cite one such instance. In the course of my research on a blood test for cancer, I was faced with a big problem pertaining to false-positive reactions. An answer was given to me, by Olga, in the key word "platelet." A week later I decided to investigate that phase with extremely gratifying results. . . .

On another occasion I was attempting to find the immunologically active fraction in a cancer experiment. I made a list of the eight fractions we were studying. This list was made in Arabic on a piece of paper which was handed to Olga to hold in her hand. You both had no knowledge as to what I was asking, since this was written in Arabic. Moreover, the results of these experiments were unknown to me and would not be known until several months later. I asked in written Arabic for the active fraction. The answer came through Olga. It was fraction "C." Several months later, this was completely verified when, by experimentation, fraction "C" was found to be the active fraction.

At this time, it might be of interest to mention the fact that not only do you get answers to questions written in Arabic, but also that you both get key words in Arabic which are relevant to the situation. For example, during this last sitting, as a result of the coming of my mother from Lebanon, practically all the Arabic synonyms to be found in the dictionary for "joy" were spoken through you both.

What is even more astounding is the pronunciation of the different Arabic words according to the different dialects, and which, in a number of cases, were convincing features of the reality of the person's identity.

For example, Olga in relating to me a conversation from an uncle of mine, whom, incidentally, I had told you nothing about, and who was a doctor in Cairo, Egypt, said a few but very distinctive Arabic words in an Egyptian dialect, which is quite unique in the Arabic language. She even got the word "Al-Kahra," which is the Arabic word for Cairo in the Egyptian dialect. . . .

In further information, presented to Curtis Fuller, publisher of *Fate* Magazine, this physician also stated:

. . . On several occasions Olga and Ambrose both used scientific terms which were very appropriate for the occasion. In other words, they would fit in very well with the scientific area of the discussion. In one instance, for example, I remember their using a scientific name of a chemical compound of which I was unaware at the time. We opened to this word later in the dictionary and we found that such a drug is a new but important addition to the *Pharmacopoeia* whose function fitted in well with the general area which was being discussed then. . . .

Arabic, as you know, is a very hard language. The pronunciation is hard, especially to the foreigner. Yet, some of the words that Olga would pronounce were clearly enunciated and, what is more remarkable, they all were given in words which, when united together, gave a clear answer to the area being discussed or the question being answered. As an example, the night that my mother arrived from Lebanon to the States, we went together to the Worrall house. . . . It is to be mentioned here that not all the words she would relay were understood by me. But, on further questioning, she would usually pick the right word from a number of related words I would give her to choose from.

. . . Words attributed to an uncle of mine, a doctor who lived in Cairo, Egypt, and who was dead a number of years ago, fitted in well with the Egyptian dialect. Among these were: (i) Pronunciation of the Arabic word for "Cairo," which is "Al-Kahra" in the Egyptian dialect, while it would be "Al-Kahira" in the Lebanese dialect. (ii) Prounuciation of the words "Bahki Ana," which means "I am talking," but which is used in the Egyptian dialect. In the Lebanese dialect this would bc "Bihki Ana."

Words attributed to my relatives who lived in rural Lebanon and were dead fitted in well with the rural Lebanese dialect. For cxample, the expression "Ayha" carries no meaning to a non-Lebanese and is not in the Arabic dictionary. It even has no meaning to a Lebanese living in the big city. Yet this same vocal expression to a Lebanese from the rural areas of Lebanon carries a good deal of connotation. It takes one to rare occasions of great festivities—marriage festivities, for example—and is synonymous with a state of happiness and joy. . . .

Words attributed to a man from the desert who was dead were spokcn in classical Arabic and had reference to things of the desert. The use, for example, of the word "Ya Akh," which means "Oh, Brother," is in classical Arabic. This same expression, when related to Olga in the Lebanese dialect on other occasions, was "Ya Khy. . . ."

Episodes of this kind of extrasensory awareness are part of the frontiers of our knowledge. The gifted individual is often criticized or held up to ridicule and denunciation. Many do not pursue their talent for fear of what other people will say or believe. It is a tragedy that this is still true today, in spite of much progress in the fields of research into how these forces work.

An example of this was a case reported by a Maryland physician. The report reads as follows:

. . . For several years, I had been attending an elderly lady who was failing gradually in health. She resisted the efforts of her friends and the few remaining distant relatives to either be hospitalized or take up residence in a nursing home. Continuing to live alone under primitive conditions, she refused to follow my advice also. As her diabetes and heart trouble made advanced inroads on her health, she became more stubborn, and refused even to take her medicine.

She was found dead in her home by a neighbor one morning, and I was summoned to the home. Reconstructing the events prior to her death and interviews with her neighbors, it was decided that she had probably died two days prior to being discovered.

I had known Olga Worrall, a clairvoyant, for several years.

The fact that I could not establish a definite time of death for my patient concerned me. Suddenly, I thought I could kill two birds with one stone by calling Olga and testing her powers by attempting to establish the time of death for my patient.

Needless to say, I was skeptical, and even tho Olga would give me the "correct" time of death, who could prove it or who would believe it? However, it was not this incidental fact that was so important.

The unasked for information that Olga, thru her clairvoyance, offered was indeed astonishing. I was talking to Olga via long distance phone. She had never seen or known of the patient under consideration. She proceeded to tell me facts about the patient, her habits and home which were easily corroborated.

Olga stated that the patient was standing beside her and had died at 7:00 P.M., two days prior. Of course there was no way of proving this. She went on that the patient had been a recluse and had a penchant for accumulating things—that she had stacks of clothing, many old-fashioned dresses reaching to her ankles, the majority of which she had not worn, that she had been living in a house without modern conveniences and alone; that a large sum of money would be found in cash in her home, that she had several bank accounts, that eventually it would be proven that her worth was thirty thousand dollars.

Indeed, while I was examining the deceased, a sum of money was found in her clothing, approximately three thousand dollars, three or four bank books of different banks were found, each containing several thousand dollars worth of entries. It was true that she had lived in a house without electricity, central heating, telephone or running water.

In the phone conversation, Olga had mentioned that the deceased's father was conveying a message that he no longer was blind as he had been in life. I, of course, had never met this man since he had been dead upwards of a quarter of a century. The remarkable thing concerning this isolated bit of information was that a distant cousin corroborated this by stating that he had been blind in his last years of life.

The last bit of proof was contained in a local newspaper six months after the patient's demise. It stated among other things that the worth of her total estate came to thirty thousand dollars. . . .

Spiritual healing operates in many ways. In its broadest interpretation, I believe one must recognize that spiritual healing is at work in every case of recovery from disease. It would be difficult to prove that spiritual healing is not being applied at the same time as medical treatment, and who will say that the hands of the Lord or the saints do not work through and with doctors and nurses and contribute to the recovery of the patient?*

There is no reason to eliminate correct medical treatment while the patient is receiving spiritual healing, for the two are complementary and compatible.

In the usual interpretation, spiritual healing connotes the restoring of a person to health *without* the assistance of medical or other treatment. However, we must face the fact that in practically every case of illness, medical or other treatment has already been administered before spiritual healing per se is tried. In the event a patient recovers when spiritual healing is added to the medical or other treatment, it may be the result of the combination of the two methods; therefore, the patient should not give all the credit to spiritual healing, which may have been only instrumental in tipping the scales in favor of recovery.

Spiritual healers should work as associates with the other healing professions. Olga and I work in harmony with the medical

* Much of this material I have drawn from lectures I have delivered to various church groups.   A.W.

profession and we pay tribute to its competence and accomplishments.

Everything in Nature is according to law. We live according to the laws of health or the laws of disease. It is impossible to break any of Nature's laws. For instance, the laws of health cannot be broken, but a person can live according to the laws of disease.

Spiritual healing is a natural phenomenon. It occurs strictly in accordance with natural laws.

There is evidence that spiritual healing power is demonstrated through people of many religions, and through some who have no religious affiliations.

Spiritual healing forces appear to be subject to spiritual, physical, and psychical laws. There seems to be an intelligence of high order behind healing manifestations. I believe that the healing power has its origin and source of supply in the Supreme spiritual power that governs and controls all things, material and immaterial, and that this type of healing is accomplished through both spiritual beings and beings in the flesh. Some would say through angels and mortals.

The importance of psychical conditions and their effect on success or failure of spiritual healing ministrations cannot be over-emphasized. With all other things being equal, two identical cases could be treated; in the one case success is assured by the proper psychical environment, in the other case unfavorable psychical conditions make success impossible. Any attempt to show that spiritual healing can be accomplished in the presence of a critical audience, or a group of unbelievers, is almost certain to fail.

This is the nature of spiritual healing.

The absence of specific knowledge pertaining to the laws governing spiritual healing gives rise to conjecture. We make an educated guess as to how this power works. Over the years I have developed a theory, a working hypothesis founded on observations of results. I will attempt to explain it in laymen's language.

It is commonly known that we are surrounded by force fields.

Gravitation is one with which we are all familiar, and there are others, such as magnetic and electrical fields, in daily use to make our modern way of life possible.

I believe there exists a field of energy, akin to life itself, around and about us. We draw our daily supply of energy from this inexhaustible storehouse.

When we insulate ourselves by wrong thinking or wrong living from this source of supply, we become sick. If we expend more energy than we take in, we become tired and listless; we are like batteries that need recharging. Rest and sleep normally are the methods used to recharge the human battery. In sickness something has interfered with the recharging, and more than rest and sleep is sometimes required to restore health.

Medical therapy may remove the interference completely or in part, and the human battery will be able to take a more or less full charge again. If medical therapy is not successful, then spiritual healing can be given as a supplementary treatment.

There is an inexhaustible supply of energy around us. Our only problem is in tapping the source of supply.

A patient is one who is unable properly to tap the source of supply. A spiritual healer is a person who is spiritually, psychically, and biologically adaptable as a conductor between the source of supply and the patient. Under the proper conditions, healing energy will flow from the source through the healer into the patient.

The healing energy can be compared with electric current. It can flow only through a suitable conductor. The conductor must be connected to the source of supply, and to the load, which in this case is the patient. The spiritual healer must be more than a simple conductor; he must act as a matching transformer, because the healing current appears to have, among other things, frequency and wave length.

The spiritual healer can be compared with a radio transmitter. The patient can be likened to a radio receiver. The healing energy flows from the transmitter to the receiver. The transmitter and receiver must be in harmonic frequency for reception to take place.

The spiritual healer has an affinity with the source of healing energy, so that the energy by which the healing is to be accomplished flows in the form of a current through what we could call the healer's equivalent of a primary circuit. A change in frequency seems to occur in the healer's body, perhaps by induction in a neural secondary circuit, then the current flows through this circuit from the healer to the patient. There is, in effect, an inner transformer that adjusts the current to the frequency that can be received by the patient. This spiritual attunement is vitally important in spiritual healing.

There are many kinds of spiritual healing, as there are many kinds of people gifted with this particular gift of God. Some prefer one technique to another. Some prefer absent treatment, some physical contact, the laying on of hands. Some prefer to work in small groups, some enjoy the stimulation of vast crowds. Unfortunately, results obtained under the emotion-charged conditions of crowds may be of a purely temporary psychological nature and these results disappear when the emotional setting is removed. The patient who thus reacted in hysterical spasm rather than through actual healing suffers the additional mental shock of realizing that he is not healed at all.

This is the great danger in all spiritual therapy in which emotionalism is too deeply stirred. Calmness, peace, gentleness, patience, waiting on the power of the Lord—these are the effective avenues. That the other roads do achieve true healing cannot be denied.

Other healers prefer the quiet of the church. Here, attendance is usually measured in hundreds instead of thousands, but the environment is more conducive to lasting healing.

In healing that involves direct physical contact the question arises: By what method could this contact be made? I believe the healing currents utilize the nervous system and that placing the hands on specific nerve centers produces the fastest results.

Healing without physical contact presents different problems.

How does the force travel over vast distances, for example? Do time, distance, and similar factors interfere?

Often, long lists of names, perhaps as many as several hundreds, are read at church healing services. This is often an exhausting experience for both the minister and the congregation. There is really no need for this kind of effort. We are reaching out to the Supreme Intelligence, omniscience itself. Since the names already have been placed before His altar in supplication, reciting the names over hardly appears called for. The experience Olga and I have had indicates that results of an affirmative nature are obtained in equal measure without mentioning or reading lists of names. It is a metaphysical force, a metaphysical knowing. However, Olga believes that for psychological reasons there are advantages in reading out these names in healing clinic procedure.

Small prayer groups, trained in healing techniques, are able to focus their attention on an individual patient and may, indeed, treat as many as ten patients effectively in an evening. Under the direction of an experienced leader such patients should be "treated" separately. A short time interval should be allowed between each case for best results.

In direct physical contact, as with the laying on of hands, often there is a tingling sensation experienced by both the healer and the patient. In healing without physical contact the experiences vary with each case and each healer. As I have already noted, in my own case the current appears to flow from the solar plexus. However, unlike the heat experienced in the laying on of hands, the current from the solar plexus appears to be cool. (Perhaps low frequency current is involved in healing with physical contact and high frequency in healing at a distance.) In both cases I experience the sensation that something similar in consistency to heavy air is leaving me.

Attitude of patient and healer is all-important. There must be complete relaxation of mind and effort. I cannot force the healing power to work, just as I could not "will" an electrical current through a wire. I cannot demand results. I cannot be impatient and I do not throw up my hands in defeat if the first experience achieves no apparent results. The greatest need is for relaxation which may be achieved with one person by using soft music, and with the next by discussing his favorite subject such as art, baseball, or electronics. The patient must be given time to conquer his own fears and to rid himself of any guilt complexes he may be entertaining.

One patient who came to me assured me that she had lived an exemplary life, but that in a previous incarnation she had committed sins for which now she was being punished by illness and suffering. Before we could begin to help alleviate her suffering, I had to make her realize how she, herself, by this attitude, could be blocking the force that could bring help.

There is no set pattern which governs success and failure in spiritual healing. There are so many variables involved that no one has gathered together sufficient statistical data to predict the chance of curing any particular disease by spiritual healing.

The question arises as to why there should be any failure in view of the fact that we are asking the intervention of the Supreme Being who is omnipotent. We could also ask why is disease in existence. The answer is that everything is accomplished in accordance with natural law.

A healer is pleased when a patient is cured of a disease. However, he takes no credit for the cure because he is just an instrument used by a higher power. When a patient is not cured, the healer should not feel that he has failed. The patient may not have been receptive, or the healer may not have been adaptable to healing that particular patient. In either case, the patient would not respond. When a cure takes place, both healer and patient can rejoice and give thanks for something that happened that neither can explain.

15 ❧ Audit

Wainwright House in Rye, New York, is a beautiful modern chateau turned into a center for the quest of truth, physical, metaphysical, spiritual. A gray-stone mansion with lovely lawns and vines, at the side of a quiet harbor, it is a restful place to which, for many years, leaders of things spiritual, including spiritual healing, have gathered to commune and confer. Olga attended all of the healing seminars held in this house, and I attended most of them. We both participated in the discussions and deliberations.

It was at Wainwright House that we first met Aldous Huxley. He was one of the speakers at the Healing Seminar.

At the breakfast table at Wainwright House a group of us were joined by Mr. Huxley. Olga was sitting to his right. We were all very much interested in what Mr. Huxley had to say concerning the program for the morning session.

During a lull in the conversation we heard Olga say to Mr. Huxley, "There is a woman by your side who gives me the name of Maria; she tells me she is your wife. She wishes to convey the following information to you:

" 'Tell him that I understood every word he said even though I was in a coma and he wondered if I were really aware of what was going on. I heard every word of the poetry that he read to me by the hour, and I am so grateful to him for all he did for me.' "

We were startled to see Mr. Huxley bow his head and wipe the tears from his eyes. He confirmed Olga's message and added, "I did indeed wonder if she heard what I was reading to her, or whether I was wasting my time. How comforting to know that she was aware of my presence."

After Mr. Huxley left the table, we were informed that Mrs. Huxley had passed on two months before.

We were to meet Aldous Huxley again, this time at Springfield College, Springfield, Massachusetts, where I am a member of the Corporate Board and where Mr. Huxley was appearing as one of the guest speakers.

Mr. Huxley, at this second meeting, recalled his experience at Wainwright House, stating that the message he had received from his wife through Olga had been a comfort to him.

We are aware that many people place their greatest interest in the more material things; they do not concern themselves to any great extent with a search for spiritual knowledge. There are those whose interest in religion is entirely passive and those whose attitude is one of tolerance. What is needed to stimulate their interest?

Perhaps the spiritual food we are serving requires the touch of the Master. What did He have in His spiritual fare that is lacking today? Was it His power to demonstrate the spiritual gifts which had been bestowed upon Him? This, I believe, is the probable answer to our question.

Before we can understand or demonstrate these spiritual powers, we must first know that the real self is spirit. Upon this foundation reason and logic will permit us to accept the possibility and probability of the existence of spiritual powers or gifts, and the demonstration of the powers will be expected as a natural occurrence accompanying the maturing of spiritual consciousness.

What becomes clear is that at a certain level there is a marriage of the physical and metaphysical laws; this reveals itself as occurring at the threshold of the nonmaterial realm where the influence of the metaphysical comes into play, making us aware of the presence of those force fields we have found in the metaphysical world.

In investigating the many disciplines used to promote healing, including those that some people have held to be diametrically opposite, they appear in their true character as merely different aspects of the same thing. For all work according to immutable laws of God—or not at all. We are not two kinds of a being, but one, and that being, in its purest essense, is spirit and of God. Therefore, it follows, too, that every atom of our being is of God. Jesus tells us this in other words: "Be ye therefore perfect, even as your Father which is in heaven is perfect."

When one becomes accustomed to the naturalness and wholesomeness of spiritual powers, all fear of the manifestation will vanish, and the exercise of spiritual gifts will not be looked upon as evidence of being in league with the dark angels—or as a mild form of insanity!

In the audit of actual healing results, records are difficult to obtain unless one keeps a true case history of each incident. Many people who obtain healing do not write or in any other way let us know. Or we may not hear about a healing until later. A woman calls us. "Don't you recall—two years ago—I wrote you about my little girl who was dying of pneumonia. Well—now, over the week-end in Vermont—skiing—she broke her leg. I'm wondering. . . ."

A minister calls to our attention a teen-age girl who is a deep psychotic, a schizophrenic. She has wild delusions and is in serious need of help. But medicine and psychiatry have done all they can for us. The minister asks me, "Do you think you could help?"

I tell him that I think we can, but he is not to mention this to her. That evening spiritual therapy is administered in absentia. A day or so later he meets her on the street. She is smiling, which is unusual for her. She is excited. She says, "I don't know what is happening to me, but *something* good is happening."

The pastor asks her, "What do you mean?"

"I feel so much better. I feel like I used to feel. Like myself again."

Ultimately, she is completely restored to what could be called mental health. Was it what we did, our treatment? Certainly, we could not prove it in a court of law. Certainly, we did nothing that could be interpreted as medical practice.

But, equally, medicine did nothing it had not been doing before. Spiritual therapy, then, was the one added factor and, following this additional force a dramatic and immediate change in her condition was observed and reported.

Failures? Of course there have been failures. Some people ask us: *Why do you not talk of those cases where healing did not result?* There are, it appears to us, several valid answers to this. One is, of course, the obvious futility of dwelling on the case that does not respond. What is one to say? I recall a case of a blind woman who came to Olga and me for help at the urging of a friend. In this case I knew at once, psychically, that the woman's optical nerves had been destroyed. (This was later confirmed by her physician.) Apart from that fact, some help might have been possible, spiritually, psychologically, emotionally, we do not know in what other ways— but the woman herself was bitter, antagonistic, angry at everyone and everything, blaming the world for her affliction. To our mind, she blocked all avenues to healing of any nature or in any measurable degree.

Percentages, I think, are more important than the individual cases to get an audit that makes sense. These figures indicate that healings of a spiritual character result in only a certain percentage of cases. Lourdes reports only an infinitesimal figure; ruled out are hundreds of healings that fail to meet extremely scientific requirements that must be obtained before a healing can be certified as a "miracle" in the terms of the church. The Christian Scientists do not give out any percentages. Certain evangelical healers have cited figures of as high as 25 per cent total healings. This does not mean that in many cases individuals are not deeply affected and helped and their condition improved. St. Stephen's Church (Episcopal), in Philadelphia, whose healing ministry under the leadership of Dr. Alfred Price has become one of the great Protestant healing shrines of the world, informed one reporter that St. Stephen's receives, according to its best estimates, "affirmative results and answers to prayer in at least 40 per cent of all its cases."

The fact that we do not hear at all from many of the thousands of cases confuses the percentile because we do know that some write later—when they need help for others—reporting then, for the first time, the healings they received.

The record sums up as follows:

1. Statistically, the figures are inadequate for any definitive answer to be given reliably, beyond the statement that some healings—dramatic and lasting—do occur, and that many other persons are helped.

2. Actually, the letters, photographs, and records which do come to us, requesting healing (and those run into many thousands), as well as those cases of healing which we work with and know personally, indicate beyond the slightest question that there is a force at work, that it can be used effectively, that some persons are more gifted in drawing on this power than others, and that it does open doors to new therapies and new concepts. Until very recently these had been either totally forgotten or overlooked by medical practitioners, but today they are becoming more and more recognized by both laymen and medical practitioners.

We are surrounded by a healing power, just as we are surrounded by magnetic fields, electricity, air, ether, and all the other forces around us that we do not see but which we are able to measure and study in various ways. The need for scientific knowledge about this field force of healing is obvious and is becoming increasingly urgent in our modern world.

At Wainwright House a number of experiments have been made to test currents flowing through the hands of recognized spiritual therapists. In my own case a piece of dental X-ray film, on which was superimposed a lead bar, was fastened to the palmar surface of my right hand with adhesive tape. This was an experiment to test whether or not the healing current that flowed through my hands in the act of healing could be recorded on X-ray film.

In this Wainwright House test, with complete voluntary co-operation of the individual involved, I was asked if I would see what help, if any, I could bring to a woman who was ill and who was at Wainwright House at that time.

I was taken into the room where this woman was waiting and told to begin my work. I was asked also if I would report the moment I felt any "power" flowing through me to this sick woman. I put my hands upon her and stated, "I feel the current starting immediately."

The force which I feel usually starts in my shoulders and comes down into my hands. It has the feeling of heat.

In this instance there was no need for a period of attunement between the patient and myself; the healing current began to flow immediately I made contact.

When the test was completed and the X-ray film developed, there was discovered on the X-ray film the appearance of a single line of light. This light had no right to be there. In only about 6 per cent of the tests of healers by this method is such a light configuration discovered.

What the power was that made this light is simply not known. It definitely was not X-ray light, I was informed by the man in charge of these tests, Dr. Julius Weinberger, an electronic scientist formerly with the Radio Corporation of America.

While we do not know, and may never know, the essential nature of this force, I am convinced that we should be able, by scientific method, to establish the laws of how it operates and in what ways it can be most effectively used.

PART III ❧ MEANINGS

Is the power available to everyone?

Until now in this story we have dealt, in large measures, with our own lives and our experiences with these spiritual forces.

Here we turn to a rather wider vista of the meanings behind these forces and events, and of their application to all of us, to all who seek to touch, by one route or another, the hem of His robe.

16 ⮞ Theory and Fact

Nothing in our lives happens without a cause—or a *modus operandi*. Nor are there any roads barred to us in our quest to understand causes and their mechanisms and chemistry.

Yet the answers, particularly in the area of spiritual healing, are deep, far-probing, and difficult.

To understand healing, we must understand cognate existence itself.

In the broadest sense, the definitions of life vary from the simple to the complex; from the spiritual to the material; from the finite to the infinite. We also find that we cannot fully explore life without encountering God.

An explanation of life can become extremely involved theologically, scientifically, and technically. We are looking at what appears to be an admixture of the finite with the infinite; an interlacement of the spiritual with the material; a mysterious union of the unseen with the seen; an interfusion of mind and soul and physical body; a merging of that which is without form, with a bodily form; a synthesis of intelligence, reasoning, sentience, instinct, intuition, emotion, judgment, volition, understanding, and a vehicle of matter. We are looking at the expression of life, and more specifically, life as expressed through man.

Life is complex and complicated, its components numerous and so combined in intricate arrangements that the mind cannot readily grasp their mutual relations; it will be necessary to look at these components separately if we are to understand anything of the nature of life.

We, of finite minds, can most easily think of human life as having a beginning. Let us assume that this beginning coincides with the moment of conception.

At conception we have a fertile egg that is microscopic in size. In twelve days' growth it is possible to differentiate the brain. This early development is at a very rapid rate. However, the rate of growth diminishes as the embryo increases in size. At the time of birth a child's weight is millions of times what the egg weighed at conception. The rate of growth continues to slow down after birth, governed by some law or intelligence, which for the moment we can call "natural."

The brain of a child at birth makes up approximately 11 per cent of the total body weight, yet in an adult it is only 2½ per cent of the total body weight. It is obvious then that the reduction in rate of growth of the brain is greater than the reduction in rate of growth of the rest of the body. This shows further evidence of intelligence or natural laws in operation.

Examination by scientists shows that the human body is composed of cells. It is estimated that a child's body, at birth, has many millions of cells while that of an adult has a correspondingly larger number.

The human body is also a form of machine. The heart is a pump with valves, the limbs have their levers and joints, the muscles are the actuators, chemical action generates heat and electrical power, and the nervous system carries the signals to control the operations. The brain can be likened to a computer, and the solar plexus is in some respects a monitor.

The physical man is therefore electromechanical in nature, but this is not all, for further research indicates man is also electronic in nature.

Scientists conducting research into the electric-electronic nature of man are known as electrobiologists. It is reported that man produces electrical outputs in the radio frequency range and is capable of detecting and translating such signals received from the outside world.

It is now being established that ionization of air, solar flares, cosmic rays, and magnetic fields all influence the mental and physical state of human beings. Tests show that there is a steady flow of direct current moving in one direction along the sensory nerves and in the opposite direction in the motor nerves.

Within the human body it appears there are biological components that function like switches, relays, resistors, transistors, capacitors, parts found in electronic circuits of radios, radars, computers, and other electronic devices.

Most of us are familiar with the medical uses of this bioelectric phenomenon. It is the force that makes possible the electro-encephalograph, the electrocardiogram and electromyography.

What is called myoelectric control is a recent major development in this vital field of bioelectricity. When a person is moving his muscles, they are responding to electrical signals sent from the brain. These signals cause an electrochemical reaction in the muscle fibers, bringing on contraction which causes movement.

Russian scientists have learned how to use this myoelectric control to move artificial limbs. The Russians describe their device as a "cybernetic forearm prosthesis activated by nerve impulses." In other words, the amputee moves his artificial hand by simply sending messages to it from his brain in the same manner as with his natural hand. The muscle signals are amplified electronically about twenty thousand times to operate the artificial hand.

We have looked at life as expressed in the human body by electricity and motion. Let us go a little further.

The English critic and classical scholar, Richard Bentley, said, "Matter and motion cannot think."

This we can agree with, yet life is expressed through matter and motion, and in the case of human beings, thinking is also expressed through matter and motion, as we have shown.

Let us look at matter. Matter is defined as physical or corporeal substance in general as distinguished from spirit, soul, mind, etc., and from qualities, actions, or conditions.

The human body is formed of matter and we know it exists. As the human body is composed of a large number of cells, let us select a single cell and examine it. We find it is composed of molecules of different substances. A molecule has been described as a group of atoms drawn and held together by what chemists term affinity; and an atom we are told is the smallest portion of an element which exhibits all properties of that element. An atom is pictured as being composed of a positively charged nucleus, surrounded by one or more electrons.

An electron, sometimes referred to as a negatron, is the smallest supposed component of matter associated with, or consisting of, an invariable charge of negative electricity.

There are other elementary particles, such as protons, positrons, and neutrons, all of which are parts of matter.

Professor Albert Einstein, in his general theory of relativity, stated that matter and energy are different aspects of something which is the source of both, that energy can be converted into matter and matter can be converted into energy.

This "something" is described as a reservoir of undifferentiated matter/energy, being neither waves nor vibrations, nor quanta, nor any other known thing. This description of the unknown is about as close as we can get scientifically.

We have taken a single cell of the human body, divided it into its smallest parts, some of which may be energy rather than matter, and these particles are so small that a layman may consider them as practically nonexistent, but we have not found that elusive element called life. Could it be that life is also a component of Einstein's mysterious something out of which all things are created, and perhaps to which all things eventually return?

Of all biological concepts few impress me as much as the idea of "the intelligence of the cell." It is saying, in effect, that not only is there intelligence in the brain but that each cell, no matter where located in the living human body, has its own intellectual powers. We are apt to connect intellect with education, so we might ask ourselves who or what educated the cell? Can we say the cell has some instinct which governs its activity? And what is instinct?

The nineteenth-century Scottish metaphysician and author, Alexander Bain, said that instinct is untaught ability.

Many philosophers look upon the instinct of animals as being in the same nature as the instinct of man, but inferior and limited.

If we look at human instinct as something different from animal instinct, we still must regard it as being independent of reasoning or instruction, a kind of built-in knowledge.

We are familiar with psychosomatic illness, the sickness brought about by the action of the mind upon the individual cells of the body, and we may ask the question, is the mind separate and distinct, acting as a ruler over these instincts? Are instincts part of the mind?

Spirit, soul, mind, and psyche are words that have caused and even now continue to cause confusion because of the many interpretations of their meanings.

Spirit is used in contradistinction to matter.

Soul is the term used for the immaterial human entity which thinks, feels, and wills. It includes intellect, emotion, and will. Soul has a more determinate meaning than spirit, being reserved for human beings, whereas spirit may be applied to other types of entities also.

Mind, in a general sense, includes all the powers of sentient being apart from the physical factors in bodily faculties and activities. Mind is more than intellect.

Psyche is a term used by many psychologists to avoid philosophical and religious connotations of the word soul. It includes the meaning of subconscious self among other meanings.

Intellect, thought, consciousness, and intuition are defined as follows:

Intellect is that assemblage of faculties which is concerned with knowledge as distinguished from emotion and volition.

Thought is the act, process, or power of thinking.

Consciousness includes all that a sentient being perceives, knows, thinks, or feels, from whatever source arising, and of whatever character, kind, or degree, whether with or without distinct thinking, feeling, or willing.

Intuition is primary knowledge antecedent to all teaching or reasoning.

Knowledge, which embraces all the mind knows, from whatever source derived or obtained, or by whatever process, is the aggregate of facts, truths, or principles acquired or retained by the mind, including the intuitions native to the mind and all that has been learned respecting phenomena, causes, laws, principles, literature, and so forth.

I have touched upon a few of the things involved in life or the expression thereof. They are not of the material world as we know it, yet without them we would not know that this physical realm exists.

Our knowledge of the material world comes through our senses, which, speaking in a physical sense, are dependent on bodily functions, but speaking in a spiritual sense, are dependent upon extrasensory faculties.

Both physical and extrasensory stimuli are received by the mind. They are electrical and electronic in nature, and the mind, acting upon the signals or information received, processes them by certain faculties and comes to conclusions resulting in decisions and actions which in turn result in phenomena which we call life.

A report, published in 1964 by the Ampex Corporation, computer manufacturers, points out the scientific approach to the investigation of thought patterns. It reads as follows:

Can an electrical pattern in the brain be identified and associated with specific behavior? That is the question a husband and wife doctor team is attempting to answer at Stanford University Hospital's

Electroencephalogram Laboratory. To aid their research, they have enlisted the facilities of a specially-built computer and two Ampex Instrumentation Recorders. . . .

Enough is understood about evoked responses in the brain to realize that they represent electrical signs of the receipt of information in local areas of cerebral cortex. Experimenters can check brain patterns before, during and after stimulation to verify what the cortex does with the information it receives. The doctors . . . gather hundreds of responses from each experiment, average them on a computer, then inspect the wave forms for patterns. . . .

A normal subject is comfortably seated in a special room where he (or she) receives visual and auditory signals. Eight EEG leads are attached to the subject's scalp at one end and to an Ampex SP-300 Instrumentation Recorder at the other. He sits quietly with eyes closed and headset on.

(I might interject here something that may be of importance to those developing clairvoyance, clairaudience, or other forms of extrasensory perception. There is a brain-wave pattern known as the alpha rhythm which is not present when the eyes are open, it is present only when the eyes are closed. Having the eyes open may have some effect on one's E.S.P.)

These experiments could lead to some very important facts of life, and perhaps of life after death.

Death, as we know it, means that physical stimuli are no longer received by the mind; therefore, the signals or information received from the material realm are not entered in the mental computer, and there is no output in a physical manner to show the presence of life by action or activity in the material body.

The mind, however, continues to receive inputs from the spiritual or extrasensory world, and to express results in a non-physical manner through a spiritual body in a way that can be observed by those able to perceive, such as persons having the gifts of clairvoyance and clairaudience.

It is possible that spiritual or extrasensory stimuli are purely electronic in nature, and that the phenomena observed in extraterrestrial realms are the expressions of life in a new dimension, yet always we are forced to recognize that beyond life is being, that which observes, reasons, thinks, judges, understands, and recalls; it is the Divine Principle which makes us a part of that which is revered as the Supreme Being, and we cannot escape the observation that man is more than electromechanical in nature.

Only an electronic spiritual concept can explain the ever-unfolding phenomena of human life.

17 ❧ Sources

What are the sources of the healing power on which we draw and how do we reach those sources? In what manner can the flow be achieved?

Two of the most important roads to these sources are meditation and contemplation. They are, in many ways, similar but they are not the same.

Meditation is a period set apart in which there is continuous application of mind and thought to the consideration of religious and moral truth. Its purpose: to promote personal wholeness, holiness, and the love of all that we mean by the word Divine.

Contemplation is one step further: the reaching through meditation to higher grounds on the metaphysical heights, the reaching of a state of rapt regard for creation. It finds in one individual selected idea, to which attention is directed, the divine essence in every quality, its virtues, its glory. It is a fullness of awareness of creation.

It is as with a child, an infant, becoming aware of the universe, awakening to his own consciousness and the memory of forces and forms separate from himself. He becomes aware of needs, desires, hunger, and sleep. He will become absorbed in his physical needs and desires, narrowing his awareness, recognizing only those things pertaining to the earth-bound existence, particularly those things concerned with source of supply and with pleasure and pain; the one he seeks to obtain, the other to avoid.

He grows up in the world. The law of self-preservation takes over in large measure. He fights for his rights, he fights to live. He becomes involved in the pleasures and treasures of the world, faced, on all sides, with the laws of man, bound in by this or that regimentation and exigency and restriction, rebelling against this or that selfishness or greediness of others—even rebelling against himself, caught in a field of confusion and seeking meaning and definition and direction in a world where the highest authorities, basing their opinions on irrefutable truths, completely contradict each other.

And often, after a long time of wandering in this personal wilderness, he appeals to God for help, for a way out, for answers. He wonders: Since God knows all things, does man need to pray out loud with vocalized prayers? Does God not hear what is in the heart of the seeker? So he begins what is in fact a form of devotion we call meditation. He seeks to reach the reality of God by reaching out for the Kingdom that Christ tells us is within ourselves.

He thinks of the attributes of God: Love, Wisdom, Mercy, Omnipotence, Omniscience, Omnipresence.*

He visualizes the majesty, beauty, and depth of a Being thus endowed. He is spiritually enlightened by a new concept of God. He is here now, and always available regardless of time and place. Doubt and fear are dispelled; there is no longer a feeling of being alone.

Here is the time, the moment, when such a man crosses the threshold into the Hall of Contemplation. He finds himself in a strange silence. The material world, including even his own body, takes on an aspect of unreality. He passes through the portal into an intuitive consciousness of the Divine Reality. Here at the threshold he touches the hem of His garment, within the Hall of Contemplation he becomes enfolded in that garment.

Continuing his contemplation by waiting alert for further knowledge, he becomes more and more aware of his affinity with the Supreme Being, until at last he reaches the realization that all

---

* Much of this section is included in a privately printed booklet I wrote in 1956 on the subject of contemplation and meditation. A.W.

are one, and the full significance of the words, "The Father dwelleth in me and I in Him," dawns upon his awakened spiritual consciousness, and he says, yes, indeed. God is "nearer than hands and feet."

These are the steps by which meditation and contemplation lead us upward, steps of prayer beyond the formal vocalized prayer to the higher plane. It is prayer here that has no words, no images, no ideas; the mind is pure, passive, nonselective; however, the consciousness is awake and alert.

A watchful, listening vigilance is maintained with an expectancy to receive impressions not generated by oneself or the mental and physical stimuli that abound on every hand, but from the Supreme Intelligence that transmits only truth and knows what one needs to know.

It is at this level, this plateau of the spirit achieved rarely in our lives and for moments only, that man of this plane of existence is one with God.

For this time, and in this way, and by such a route he dwells, in such periods, between two worlds, two places of existence.

Meditation and contemplation may be looked upon as keys used by a healer to open the doors to spiritual knowledge to turn on the healing current, and to bring into focus that which God is ready to reveal through the use of spiritual gifts.

The healer waits upon the intuition. He may receive an impression, clairvoyantly, by clairaudience. This is achieved only in certain individuals, and often only after many years of effort and study and spiritual development. For some, the gifts are strong from the beginning. But, in all cases, it should be thoroughly understood by the healer, that with the gifts come responsibilities.

But the intuition comes; it is primarily in intuition that the healer receives his guidance. A woman came to me because of a severe pain in the calf of her leg.

In the treatment, I ran my hand over her and stopped at her thigh. Intuitively, I sensed that there was something like the point of a needle cutting into the nerve at that point.

I told her this. The patient, a former nurse, stated, "But the pain is not in my thigh. It is in the calf of my leg."

I said, "I am not concerned where the pain is felt. The cause of the trouble is in the thigh and requires surgery."

She did not believe me. She went to Walter Reed Hospital. Physicans there, after examining her, found by means of X-ray a piece of shrapnel where I had indicated. (She had been wounded in a battle area, but the presence of the fragment of shrapnel had not been detected at that time.)

The shrapnel was removed; the pain in the calf of her leg disappeared.

Intuition is a two-edged sword. Misunderstood, misinterpreted, misused, it could do harm. The healer is not to replace the physician in diagnosis; the healer may say, "The trouble is in the thigh," but it is the doctor who must confirm this and take medical action.

Intuition is the searchlight that points a way. It is not a roadmap, a defined plan of action, not a course that can be relied upon for definitive action. It is the indication of an area to be explored —with care and wisdom and responsibility.

Prayer is a key to the source of power.

We have already touched upon two kinds of prayer, meditation and contemplation.

The prayer of petition and the prayer of affirmation are both most effective when one petitions or affirms the achieving of help or healing on behalf of someone else, not the petitioner or the affirmer.

There is also prayer that is not usually considered as prayer. I refer to the prayer that is thought itself. All our thoughts, all our conscious thinking, is in essence a part of prayer.

For as a man thinketh, so he is. Indeed, as he thinketh, so he prays.

Millions of people, in many varieties of religions, pray—without thought, without purpose, reciting empty words that no longer have meaning to the one mouthing them because he does not listen to them himself, with his mind or heart or soul; he mumbles them with vague meaningless mumblings.

In mere thoughtlessness there can be no prayer. Yet the converse of this is also true: *Every thought is a prayer.*

In healing, the essence of the thought may achieve in an instant where a thousand verbalized entreaties fail. This is not because no one is listening, but because we, perhaps, ask amiss, because we are dealing not with whim but with universal law.

Too often the parrotlike repetition of phrases learned in various religious services fails to reach the source of power. Occasionally an impulsive human word or words become metamorphized by inner meaning into true prayer—and true healing. I like to cite, as an example, the story of a woman who, it appears, entirely involuntarily during a healing service uttered one word: "God."

She had been suffering from a severe rash on one arm. Physicians did not understand the cause of it and had been unable to get rid of it.

But the moment she spoke that single word the rash vanished. In a single second!

The deep meaning with which she uttered it, the surrender of self to the all-embracing Being, turned the spoken word into a full and extraordinarily effective prayer.

And, indeed, she did not need actually even to utter the word. It could have been merely in her mind—one thought, one prayer.

Whether or not we go to church regularly, we still lead prayerful lives, though we may not know it. If we wish a man sick—it is a prayer, but a prayer for sickness, not good. If we think ill of him—it is a prayer, again of evil. If, in our mind, we see him in failure—it is a prayer for his failure. If we see him healthy, successful, if we think of him in terms of love, if we surround him and his family in our thoughts with love—this is prayer. Whatever we think about others, about ourselves, our world, becomes a prayer for or against others, for or against ourselves, for or against our world.

So when we ask ourselves how we should pray, our question perhaps ought to be, How shall we think?

In true prayer our thinking is an awareness that we are part of this Divine universe. Our thinking reaches out, it has power. Prayer is a dynamic sending out of a wish, a desire, a dream in the process of realization, a plan, a hope, a need, a striving. It may be, in fact, the visualization, in picture form, of the condition desired. But it must be also imbued with the spirit of compassion and love of God.

How do we pray? Do our prayers verbalize complex thoughts? I think they should. At night, at our nine o'clock prayer time, I pray not only silently but also in vocalized prayer. Olga writes down some of these prayers as I say them.

Most of these prayers are affirmations. Typical is the following:

We feel the power and direction of Thy Spirit, Dear Father, as we come to Thee in prayer. We are clothed in the peace of Thy Holy of Holies, and we are merged in Thee, and through this Holy alliance is made possible the working of miracles and the healing of the sick.

Many have turned to us this night expecting to receive. We are thankful for this privilege of serving them and we give Thee our thanks for each one who receives. Amen.

Not one of these prayers is studied out or worked over. The words come to me in the darkness, in the time of quiet meditation. I do not know how they come exactly; the words and sentences and meanings take their own shape and pattern and form.

This is what I mean by the "source" that flows to us and through us, using us as its channel to the world.

One of the prayers out of this collection seems to me to sum up this meaning:

Father, we find ourselves again closeted with Thee in the halls of wisdom and attuned to the harmonial philosophy of Thy spirit. We feel ourselves in the company of kindred souls and we are supported by the unity of their combined uplifting force. Truly we are in the presence of the Angels of Light and together as a united band we seek to do Thy will. We are imbued with the power of Thy Spirit and the wisdom of the ages, and we shall be guided aright as we follow the dictates of Thy Spirit in service to mankind.

Thy divine power flows in us and through us, bringing blessings into the lives of others who have turned to Thee and are ready to receive. They shall receive and the results will glorify Thy name in the great works wrought by their faith that has made them whole. For these blessings we give our thanks. Amen.

18 ᓚ Procedure

Charisma derives from a Greek word meaning "gift." The charismatic healer in terms of spiritual therapy is one who has a special gift, a power that he or she can use to heal others.

Can only those who are gifted heal? This is like asking, Can a person who is not particularly gifted as an artist learn to paint? The answer is: Of course he can. Not perhaps in the measure of those described as masters of art, but often to a far greater degree than the individual himself may have thought possible. The same thing is true in the field of spiritual healing. The degree of *charisma* may be slight or great, it may be latent, it may be developed or undeveloped, trained or untrained, primitive or sophisticated. It may utilize the sacraments; Dr. John Ellis Large, for many years the pastor of New York's City Church of the Heavenly Rest, began his career in that church by calling off the previous pastor's established weekly healing service. The parishioners themselves told Large that he had no right to abolish this service, whether he believed in spiritual therapy or not. A man of deep faith, Dr. Large at once began a study of the subject and inaugurated services involving pastoral counseling with the sacrament of the Eucharist. Gifted or not, Dr. Large became one of the leading practitioners of healing of this kind—and many individuals reported to him that they had been helped and, in many cases, completely healed.

There are five basic principles which anyone moving into this field must understand and accept. Actually, many physicians, knowingly or not, have utilized one or more of these principles in addition to their regular medical therapy.

The first is that spiritual healing is not in opposition to medicine. It works with medicine, with the physician. To pray for healing is not to practice medical arts. To make an individual aware that he has Divine love and infinite healing power available to him does not relieve the individual from the necessity of observing physical and medical laws as well as spiritual; they are different aspects of the same thing.

Accepting the psychical and the physical laws, we reach out to the metaphysical. We come with the specific force of our own awareness of spiritual power, and this awareness is therapeutically brought to bear through sacrament, through the actual laying on of hands, through prayer, through affirmation.

The second basic principle is that the spiritual therapist has no power of his own. Even with those who are extremely gifted, the gift is not a gift of power itself but of the ability to be used by the power, to direct, to channel the power to others.

We are the electronic computer and reactor—the spiritual power is the source of healing energy.

The third basic principle is that we can and we must learn the art of allowing this power to work through us. This is therapeutic technique, but it is not a technique of *res medica*. It is a learning to make a contact with a force, to be receptive to the forces around us, to the impression that comes, to the inspiration, to the knowing.

Fourth, we must care. We must care for others deeply and urgently, wholly and immediately; our minds, our spirits, must reach out to them with whatever we have to bring them in the form of help and succor, without desire on our part for personal gain or private glory.

A fifth principle in spiritual therapy is the importance of the attitude of the individual who seeks healing. The person who is openly hostile certainly makes it extremely difficult for the spiritual therapist to achieve. Whatever force field can be established is bound to be made ineffective by this kind of overt antagonism.

Honest skepticism is different from hostility. A man may say, as one did to me, "I don't believe in any of this myself. But if it can help my wife, then I am for it, then I am ready to believe it."

In that instance the doctors had given up all hope for the wife, and the fact that she was cured completely won the man over to belief in spiritual therapy as an actual fact.

He became a friend of spiritual therapy because he would let nothing, not even his own deep skepticism, impede help that might come to his wife.

The patient must, in his turn, accept the obligation to allow healing to work. He must not go running off on his own tangents whenever some new possibility crops up.

A case which I reported at one of the spiritual healing seminars at Wainwright House concerned a forty-nine-year-old man who had had major exploratory surgery which revealed a malignant tumor. The cancer had developed to a point where removal of the tumor was impossible and all the surgeon, who was his brother-in-law, could recommend was that the man be given drugs for relief of the pain—and, in effect, wait in agony for death.

Here is the kind of case that often comes to the spiritual healer. There is no hope, nowhere to turn, nothing further to do, so the spiritual healer is truly the last resort, the last stop before the tomb. That is the attitude. That is also why many cases do not respond. They come in extremes and in this frame of reference.

I was asked to give him spiritual treatment. This I did. The man responded slowly but he did respond. He felt better, he reported. And he began to gain weight, a reversal of the entire process that had been going on. He gained three pounds. His physician was delighted with these results, and, whether he believed in this technique of spiritual therapy or not, he advised the man to continue with these treatments.

The patient then read a magazine article that described a new technique which employed beta rays and which reportedly had cured two individuals of the same kind of tumor.

The patient went to his doctor: could he have treatments with this new device? The doctor urged him not to do so until some check had been made on the accuracy of the reports and the permanence of the results. The patient decided otherwise and began to take treatments using the beta rays.

Instead of getting better, he grew worse and finally became so bad that the physician ordered him to cease these X-ray treatments. I saw him again and was shocked at the incredible change. He looked like a skeleton; his skin had been burned over an area about five inches in diameter by the rays. The pain he was suffering was so intense that he had to have constant heavy sedation.

Within three weeks this man was dead.

I cannot say that we could have saved him. I can say that his taking this perverse course, against his doctor's wishes, completely neglecting the fact that he had, with spiritual therapy, at least made a start in the right direction, made it impossible for us to reach him after that. He had blocked out the possibility of help.

One's time and energy are limited. The therapist must decide where and under what circumstances he can do the greatest good. He or she learns from experience under what conditions he or she can be most helpful. We have found that for some individuals the most effective treatment can be given by having them join our prayer time at nine each night. In this way they join with us, with hundreds of others, in the great metaphysical healing pool.

I consider very carefully whether I can or should take on a "case." Olga does also. We want to make sure that we are using our time to the best advantage for ourselves, for the patient. We have only so much time available. I have six basic criteria when considering whether I should take a case. These are:

1. Whether I actually have the time available for this particular case.

2. The severity and urgency of this case in relationship to other applicants who are also seeking help, where the time factor is important.

3. The degree of "affinity" between myself and the patient, in terms of spiritual values.

4. The spiritual response or urge within myself to the case.

5. The type of treatment needed, in spiritual terms.

6. My own energy level. (While spiritual healing does not drain physical strength, the need to begin with a measure of energy, both physical and spiritual, is important.)

Procedures used in direct relationship with the patient involve emotional, physical, and spiritual steps building to the concept of total healing of the whole man.

These procedures include the following:

1. Education regarding habits and posture.

2. Education regarding basic theories about the available healing force, the need for receptivity to healing, the affinity between the healer and the patient.

3. "Tuning in" technique—waiting until the patient and I are on the same "wave length," until I have become attuned to his wave length so that the force can flow.

4. Massage.

5. Laying on of hands.

6. Passes of the hands with light contacts.

7. Treatment of the patient, but by prayer and affirmation, without contact. (Subjectively, there may be merely a complete personal affirmation of truth, followed by allowing my thoughts or being to drift free in the field of consciousness itself, aware subconsciously all this time that the power is at work.)

8. Treatment without the patient having any awareness that I am giving him treatment.

9. Explanation of what treatment I am using and why.

10. The use with the patient of our definition of faith: *"Faith is the lack of resistance to that which you hope to receive."*

In all of this, I follow these rules: I do not ask for or accept remuneration. I do not seek to pry into the individual's personal business, or his religious affiliation. I do not seek to instill distrust of his physician or discourage medical treatment. I do not tell the patient he must believe in me or in my theories. And I do not, in any way, shape, or form, practice hypnosis.

In the silence I seek attunement with the patient. His spirit and my spirit are part of the universal, and I seek to harmonize them, to merge them completely. Spiritual being reaches out to spiritual being. The patient is relaxed, his whole physical, mental, and emotional state is at ease, restful, receptive; he is breathing lightly, easily, all problems and all difficulties for a moment being in a state of hiatus.

In such a moment the Spirit also transmits to me information I must have regarding treatment, placing of hands, massage, whatever is required. I must be, like the patient, receptive to these forces and facts and ready to act knowingly and certainly.

The location of the healing room is also important. There are certain places—rooms—that seem to hold the magnetic charge of the life force, the essential *élan*.

The location of a home or a room for healing, wherever possible, should be a scene, a setting of peace and contentment, soothing and relaxing. There should be no irritants in the area, no fumes or smoke, no disturbing noise, no disagreeable smells, or similar distractions. True, these are physical things but they can lead to unpleasant reactions, to destructive thoughts that reach from the mind to the emotions and to the spirit. Such a place should have a relaxing chair or couch for the patient. The light should be soft. Then, once the silence begins, the force is quickly experienced. Healing can occur and treatment can be given— emergency first-aid spiritual treatment—under any conditions, actually. But I am writing here of a permanent healing room.

The healer himself should be relaxed and should be seated with both feet firmly on the floor. Relaxation should not include crossing the legs or slouching in the chair. But be restful. Be at ease. Be at peace.

Wait upon the power.

19 &ᴥ Outreach

Over the years this voluntary ministry which Olga and I began decades past has continued.

But always it remains the individual and his need—and the individual impression—which seems to us important.

And it is not all grim or foreboding; it is also gay and full of love and of joy in this our present world.

I recall one evening at the dinner table when Olga said to me that before the Thanksgiving season was upon us, I would have to get myself a new secretary, as Shirley, the young lady I had, would be leaving to get married.

I told her that this was all very well as a prediction of things to be, but that before a girl could get married, she had to have some young man seriously interested in her and that my secretary worked too hard and had no time for such things. So far as I knew, she had no boyfriends.

Olga said, "All right, dear. But—if anything *does* happen, just remember that I warned you."

A month later Shirley telephoned Olga and asked if she might stop over in the evening. "I have a letter I want you to hold," Shirley said. "I want to see what might come through to you about the letter. I hope you don't mind."

Olga agreed. When Shirley arrived at our home and was seated, she handed Olga an envelope. Olga took the envelope and held it some seconds. She then told Shirley, "This envelope contains another envelope inside. And the other envelope contains a picture of your future husband."

"But that isn't possible," Shirley said, smiling. "All right—it is the picture of a man. But I just met him. We've only had two dates so far."

Psychically, through Shirley's deceased grandmother, word was given to Olga that the next time Shirley had a meeting with the young man, he would present her with a solitaire diamond ring. Further, the engagement would be only a week long; they would be married before Thanksgiving.

All of this sounded so preposterous to Shirley that she absolutely refused to accept the possibility of its being true. But on Monday morning she came into the office with stars in her eyes and a solitaire diamond ring on the third finger of her left hand.

Shirley told me that my wife had been correct about everything except the time of the wedding. They would not be married until the Christmas holidays when her husband-to-be would be on leave from the army.

Two days later Shirley came to me in great excitement. Her fiancé's army assignment had been changed; she wanted to know if she could possibly have the rest of the week off because they were going to be married on Saturday, the week before Thanksgiving.

The wedding took place at the time foreseen by Olga clairvoyantly. They are now happily married with home and children of their own.

There have been many moments of lightness and joy. But not all of the results of our reaching out through ministry have been entirely unmixed with serious reactions and unlooked-for developments.

Neither Olga nor I was prepared for one incredible situation which began for us on a Sunday morning in the spring of 1955.

We were awakened early with a long-distance call from a woman in New Jersey. She stated that she was suffering from an incurable disease, and she wanted to make an appointment with me for healing.

Olga said that this was not possible; I was a businessman, not a professional healer. I was not available for private healing. While we are willing to help, we do have to make some limitations; otherwise, we could not do anything else from morning to night and night to morning again.

The woman then told Olga that she had read about us in a story in the morning paper.

Olga told her that we would remember her in the nine o'clock prayer hour and would she join with us in that hour wherever she happened to be at that time. The woman thanked Olga and hung up.

A moment later there was another phone call. It was someone else seeking healing for tuberculosis. This call was from New York. The same routine was followed as in the first call. We wondered what had been said in that Sunday paper. Other calls followed swiftly; the phone was ringing constantly. There was no letup.

I told Olga, "I don't know what it is—but something has happened."

I recalled that we had been interviewed some months earlier by the distinguished American author, Will Oursler, who was at that time preparing a book on religious healing. The book was not scheduled for publication for some months, however. We did not see how this could have anything to do with the situation.

The calls kept coming. I brought in the Sunday paper that was on the front porch. We immediately looked through it to see if there were any mention made of us that should be causing this outbreak of interest in the Worralls.

At last, in the supplement known as the *American Weekly*, we found it; some of the material from Will Oursler's forthcoming book had been condensed into a series of articles. Sure enough, in one of them there was a mention of our ministry. It also mentioned the New Life Clinic. It was only a few paragraphs, most of this article of the series being given over to other forms of spiritual therapy.

On the Monday morning following we received a call from Dr. Day. He was astounded; hundreds of calls were coming into the church as a result of the article in the paper.

We both agreed that the telephone calls were a remarkable response to what was no more than perhaps half a dozen paragraphs for both our work and that of the clinic. But we were not too disturbed; the response would subside in a few days at most. We went off that afternoon on a social visit, a long-standing date that we could not break. On our return the neighbors were waiting. Long-distance operators had been calling them, trying to reach us. Some of the calls came from as far away as Alaska and Hawaii. Nothing like this had ever happened before to us or to the neighborhood.

This weekly magazine, of course, was distributed through scores of newspapers in all parts of the country, in fact of the world, and reached as many as twenty to twenty-five million people.

We were to learn how important *this* outreach was when mail began to arrive the next day. It came not in the handful of letters we usually receive—perhaps twenty or thirty. The first day it reached perhaps two or three hundred. That was only the beginning. The number of letters climbed in the next few days to almost five hundred a day. The post office began to deliver the mail in bundles.

The local postmaster telephoned, wanting to know what was going on. Olga told him the story and he, in turn, offered full co-operation by putting a "flag" on our address at the post office. Our mail carriers and special delivery clerks deserve a vote of thanks for the way they have forwarded letters, even to this day —many without the correct address, some envelopes containing only "Ambrose Worrall, Healer," no street or city or state.

So great was the influx of letters, telegrams, phone calls, and packages (photographs of individuals seeking help, including life-size oil portraits on occasion) that we had to deal with it immediately, forthrightly, and compassionately. Friends came in to lend a helping hand; they knew we had no secretarial help at home and so they pitched in, opening mail, with Olga answering the letters. What we did was to urge them all to join us in a redesigned, reshaped nine o'clock prayer hour, at which time we would deal with their needs.

Just answering the letters was an overwhelming assignment in itself. But with the help of these kind friends, we began to get it done. The letters, we thought, would begin to drop off in a week or two. We were mistaken. Within two months, the total had reached about ten thousand, and they continued to come in at about two hundred a day. It was a constant, wearing flow.

Olga called Will Oursler to tell of these happenings which his article had brought down upon us. Will thought when she first called that we were upset because he had written only a few paragraphs about us. "Olga, I'm doing a whole chapter in the book about you and Ambrose," he said.

Olga said, "I understand, Will; I know that you didn't intend—"

"I certainly didn't intend to slight you or Ambrose," Will broke in hurriedly, still apologetic. "In fact, I've already received about fifty letters to be forwarded to Ambrose and they're still—"

That was too much for Olga. "You've got fifty letters, Will?" she said. And before he could answer, "You've got fifty—we've got ten thousand! We are swamped. We don't have room to stand up in. Our phone is ringing day and night. All our friends are pitching in to help us just to open the mail. What has that article done to us?"

Will was delighted. "Isn't that wonderful, Olga! Think of it. Ten thousand letters! And when the book comes out—we'll double that."

It was understandable that he was excited by this response to his article. And he was right about the book drawing that many more—I think the total we have received since then from people who remember that article (and strangely they were still referring to it a decade later) has reach over twenty-five thousand letters.

From this influx of human beings crying out for need, the nine o'clock prayer time became a very urgent and vital part of the overall ministry.

In the course of time we began to get other letters, from those who had written earlier asking for help and who were writing to thank us for healing which they reported they had received.

I would say we have had from three hundred to three hundred and fifty such healings reported by phone or in writing.

And although it was a slightly jolting experience when the deluge first came upon us, we are deeply grateful. It has done so much to expand our own outreach, to bring God's healing love to so many more than we could have reached by any other way.

Each step leads to the next in our lives.

Two months before Dr. Day's retirement, in 1957, Olga noticed a young man in the congregation at the New Life Clinic services. She saw around him a very unusual glow, his aura was very bright. It seemed to her he was very interested in spiritual healing.

He came each of the following three weeks, but each time slipped out just before the end of the service, so that Olga had no chance to speak to him. However, the next week he did stay behind after the healing service and introduced himself to her. He was the Rev. Robert G. Kirkley, he said, of the Mt. Washington Methodist Church in Baltimore.

He said he would like to start a New Life Healing Clinic in his church. Would she be willing to help him to get it started? She told him that she had already started several of these healing clinics in other churches and would be very glad to help him. The following week she went to his church and formally opened another New Life Clinic.

When Dr. Day was ready to retire, he was informed that the incoming minister was not interested in healing and that the New Life Healing Clinic would have to cease at the Mt. Vernon Place Church. The Rev. Mr. Kirkley, on hearing this, invited Olga to join him at the clinic in his church, an invitation she happily accepted.

It was, again, the working out of God's will for healing, I am sure; there were scores of individuals who came to the Mt. Vernon Place clinic regularly who transferred to the Mt. Washington Church. Nothing was lost, and no one seeking spiritual healing left without help.

In a brochure Olga prepared for the ministry on the technical procedures indicated in launching and conducting a healing clinic, she declares at one point:

It is important that the minister or lay worker make it clearly understood that no one can promise a healing. A healing shrine is an experimental laboratory. The minister or lay worker and the congregation or group are joining forces in trying to create the right atmosphere for holding communion with God through Christ, in the hope that if every condition is met a healing may take place. Instantaneous healings are extremely rare, so don't expect them. And above all, don't be disturbed if nothing happens for weeks or months . . . remember that healing takes place in God's time and not man's time. . . .

The healing work goes on, at the clinic and in our home.

One of our friends, a Methodist minister with a church in southern Virginia, wrote to us some summers back about his wife who had had an operation that day for cancer. The entire breast was removed. He asked us to hold a prayer service for his beloved wife. Olga did this at the Mt. Washington Church clinic. We also held her in prayer at our nine o'clock prayer hour.

Ten days later we had word from this minister that his wife had experienced healing so quickly and completely that it astounded physicians in charge. "The doctors at the hospital," he wrote, "were amazed at her miraculous recovery overnight, as it were, and we had some lengthy discussions about this spiritual healing over coffee in the hospital snack bar. It jarred some of the doctors . . . since they were in on the whole story. . . .

"Elsie is of course quite weak yet and needs to build up her strength, but she is making rapid progress. Shall I continue the laying on of hands . . . ?"

The laying on of hands had been part of the instructions Olga sent to him. He did continue, at her advice, the laying on of hands and his wife's healing also continued to progress until she was completely recovered and able to leave the hospital.

Was this just an ordinary recovery—or the working out of the healing forces to effect complete recovery far more swiftly than was considered probable or even possible in this case?

The woman's husband, though a minister, was not a healer. He had studied it a little but, like so many others, was doubtful and even skeptical of results. But he writes, "I have a strong feeling that this was God's dramatic way of convincing me of the power of prayer and the reality of the power of spiritual healing. I was timid . . . now I feel very strongly about it and want to render the most useful service I can in this field."

We can all be channels. This is what the evidence indicates.

20 ❧ From Distant Stars

This is the story of our work.

We do not know why we were selected for this ministry, for these gifts which we have tried to use, to the fullest of our understanding, only for the good of others, only to help, only to heal.

There does appear to have been, it seems to us, a pattern, a plan, to our lives, to the seeming chances that brought us together from so many thousands of miles apart, that led our lives down these paths we have followed.

Perhaps the very everydayness of our lives is part of the reason. We are not set apart from the world, we are not cloistered, we are not mystics in some remote temple, beyond the noise and bustle and daily harassment of the crowded city streets. In this any-day pattern we have been close to people of all kinds, close to their needs, close to their spiritual hunger, close to their prayer.

For these things we are grateful, for this opportunity that has been ours.

Above all, we are grateful for the opportunity to watch the power of the Holy Spirit at work in the everyday world of so many men and women and children.

The great healing power of the Holy Spirit is around us and available to us in church, in our homes, in a taxicab or a gasoline station or a hospital room—wherever the need is, one can reach out to this power.

If we cannot touch the undying flame, we can, in any case, draw near its Divine warmth that reshapes and rebuilds and restores.

This is the deepest meaning of our ministry.

&ampersand; Appendix A

Statements Regarding Personal Experiences
in Spiritual Healing

The letters and statements that are presented here have been selected, not essentially as testimonials of healing, but rather as examples out of many of the hundreds of letters the authors have received over more than thirty-five years' experience.

TO WHOM IT MAY CONCERN: To fulfill a request of Mrs. A. A. Worrall of June 8, 1959, in regard to comments made during a clergy-physicians' meeting where Dr. Price of Philadelphia spoke at the Church of Epiphany, Baltimore, Md.

Gentlemen, I am a physician whose training and experience has been in the field of General Surgery, which specialty, I practiced for 3 years. I am board-eligible, but not board-qualified.

After 5 years of intensive and meticulous study in the area of "healing" it seems to me that there is "something here" which needs greater study and illumination. Let me give you an example: In 1956 or so, a nurse who was psychiatrically oriented, consulted me for the problem of abdominal lympho-sarcomatosis. The diagnosis was made microscopically by men trained at Cancer Memorial in New York City. Therefore, we must consider the idea that the diagnosis was "probably" accurate. At any rate, the nurse believed the diagnosis and was given therapeutic dosages of X-ray therapy and that was followed with adequate amounts of nitrogen mustard therapy.

When we saw her, she had lost weight from about 140 to 106 or so; she had a tumor as large as your head in her abdomen—visible to the naked eye. She was getting 200—mgm. of Demerol 3 to 4 times a day for severe pain and was "existing" on a liquid diet. The husband's mother and father cared for the 3 children, all girls, while they were under our care.

For a week, intensive, specific "spiritual therapy" was administered to the woman and her husband on a 3-hour per day basis. Following this, she was free of pain at the end of the week and was able to tolerate a semi-solid diet.

Acting upon "inner-guidance," the suggestion was made that she and her husband stop at a "healing service" held each Wednesday morning at the Mt. Vernon Methodist Church, at that time under the auspices of the Rev. Mr. Albert Day, assisted by my friend, Mrs. Olga Worrall.

The couple followed the advice. The woman felt guided to approach Mrs. Worrall, who without any type of suggestion, was guided to "lay hands" upon the nurse's abdomen.

While no objective phenomena were noted, the nurse reported that she had "the sensation of a big cork-screw turning in my stomach." They went on their way back to New Jersey—the tumor still obviously present.

She gradually returned to her professional duties. Her visit occurred in May, as I remember, and by November, the tumor was completely gone. She has returned for follow-up checks on several occasions and is completely well.

Since that time, she has undertaken additional college work, and greater professional responsibilities than she had ever faced before her illness.

The man who did her X-ray diagnostic work and therapy even approached her and asked that she submit to further X-ray diagnosis in an effort to determine what had occurred. She did, and he was unable to find any remains of pathology.

Gentlemen, I submit to you. SOMETHING has happened here. If we are to demand homage and respect from the public-at-large in the role of guiding public and personal health policies, it is also our obligation, in my opinion, to make an honest and scientific effort to understand this phenomenon and co-operate with it to the best of our ability. Thank you for your attention.

(Signed) H. T. C., M.D.

March 30, 1961

Testimonial of a Healing
—by Charlotte J. Stout

On Tuesday, July 19, 1960, I visited Dr. — — . . . for the purpose of a checkup. Dr. — — discovered a lump about the size of a quarter in my right breast. . . . The diagnosis was confirmed and, at that time, arrangements were made for me to enter Women's Hospital on August 3.

I spoke to Mrs. Worrall on Thursday, July 21, at the New Life Clinic about the findings of the doctors and she suggested that I come to see Mr. Worrall. On Friday, July 22, I visited Ambrose Worrall and was with him in the healing room for two hours. His first impression was to feel my spinal column. He discovered a severe curvature of the spine which impaired the normal function of the nerves leading to the breast. Mr. Worrall felt there would be more trouble if this weren't corrected and asked me to make up my own mind about the hospital appointment. He was sure that an operation was not the answer. After prayerful consideration, I decided to cancel the hospital appointment and my husband was in complete agreement.

On July 24, I wrote a letter . . . cancelling the operation.

On Monday, July 25, I received another treatment from Mr. Worrall. Upon examination, Mr. Worrall found that the lump had moved and had become mobile. He was very pleased at my response to the treatment.

I continued to go to Mr. Worrall for treatments once a week for about two months. On or about October 7, I was told by Mr. Worrall that the lump had completely dissolved and no further treatment was necessary.

No further examination was made until February of 1961 when my family physician . . . examined me and found no evidence of the lump.

(Signed) Charlotte J. Stout

September 3, 1959

TO WHOM IT MAY CONCERN:

On August 18, 1959 Dr. D. C. W. came to my office complaining of pain in his lower spine, which he has had for many years. He had been to many doctors, trying to get help, but no one has been able to help him.

Upon physical examination of the patient I found a rotary scoliosis of the dorsal spine and a compensatory curvature of the lumbar spine. Severe pressure and pain in the atlanto occipital region, and the left leg ½" shorter than the right, rigidity of the abdominal musculature and paravertebral muscular tension.

After I had made my diagnosis Dr. D. C. W. told me that a lady by the name of Olga Worrall had told him the exact same thing; she also told him that he had a fall from a swing when he was very young. He told me that this was also true. She had told him exactly where his pain was, when it had happened, how it was caused and what to do to have it corrected. I treated Dr. D. C. W. from my own physical findings and from the advice of Mrs. Worrall. After the treatment, the patient felt fine and since then has not had a pain at all.

I believe that Mrs. Worrall has a valuable gift to see and detect a person's problem that we as doctors are not always able to do.

Sincerely,
(Signed) Dr. R. K. Adolph

July 7, 1960

TO WHOM IT MAY CONCERN:

In August, 1959, I came to Mrs. Ambrose A. Worrall at the New Life Clinic at Mount Washington Methodist Church and told her that my husband was ill and that the family doctor didn't know what was wrong with him. As I talked to Mrs. Worrall she kept silent, then said, "I know what is wrong with your husband, he has a congested gall bladder, spasm of the gall duct and there are a few stones in the bladder, but with proper diet and prayer he will be all right.

The family doctor insisted that my husband go to the hospital for tests and X-rays. Still no medical diagnosis. I then asked Mrs. Worrall to phone my doctor and tell him what her diagnosis was, but she refused. I then asked her if she would mind talking with the doctor if I had him call her. She said she would talk with him only if he phoned her. I asked my doctor to call her. After several days he did telephone Mrs. Worrall. She told him her diagnosis, he promptly hung up on her.

The doctors at the hospital examined my husband. They finally said that he had cancer of the pancreas, that the X-rays showed the mass, and that his life wasn't worth a nickel, and that they would have to operate on him. I called in a Hopkins doctor who made the same diagnosis. All this time Mrs. Worrall insisted that her diagnosis was correct and that if they did operate they wouldn't find cancer, but a congested gall bladder.

My husband was operated on. As soon as the operation was over the surgeon came out to the waiting room where I was and told me to take that gloomy look off my face, that my husband did not have cancer, and that when they made the big incision they found nothing wrong with the pancreas, then they made an incision for the gall bladder and found just what Mrs. Worrall said they would find, a congested gall bladder, and a large stone that had shattered into three pieces and that at the next gall spasm the stones would have been ejected, but as a precautionary measure they removed the gall bladder.

My husband came home from the hospital much sooner than is normal for such an operation, two incisions had to heal. Several weeks later, my husband went back to the hospital for a checkup and all the doctors can't figure out how they could have made such a wrong diagnosis; they rechecked the X-rays and tests, and still can't figure out what happened.

I know that prayers healed my husband and that Mrs. Worrall knew what she was talking about. My husband is back at work and enjoying good health. The Heavenly Father surely heard our prayers.

Sincerely yours,
(Signed) Estella Snyder
(Mrs. Clarence Snyder)

April 5, 1957

Dear Mr. Worrall,

Last month I had the pleasure of an extremely pleasant and informative conversation with you. As you may recall, after discussing the duties and responsibilities of a procurement evaluator, we went on to talk about your extraordinary healing powers.

I mentioned the type of affliction my mother was suffering from and requested that you find in your already overcrowded schedule a moment to think about her.

When I returned to New York, I discussed all this with my mother and also asked her to focus her thoughts on you at 9:05 P.M. She did this for several weeks to no avail; however, Wednesday night she repeated the above and suddenly felt an exhilarating sensation through her body. Her joints, which have given her excruciating pain off and on for over twenty years, felt strong and relieved.

She immediately phoned to tell the good news. I knew you would be pleased to hear that your prayers have borne fruit, and so I am rushing this off to you. Words cannot express our feelings of gratitude and appreciation. You know how grateful we must feel. . . .

Respectfully and gratefully yours,
(Signed) R. D.

September 3, 1954

In 1934, when I was six years old, I was taken by my parents to Mr. Worrall for spiritual healing. I had been ill for three years during which time my weight had remained at forty-two pounds. Our family doctor was not able to cause any improvement in my condition and advised my parents that he was unable to discover what was the cause of my ailment, to feed me just candy and not to worry about my lack of appetite but to prepare themselves for my passing, because I was suffering from the same ailment that caused the passing of my brother and sister.

After Mr. Worrall began to give me healing, I began to gain weight, was able to go back to school, and participate in normal activities that up until then were denied me.

A number of years had passed from the time that I had been healed through Mr. Worrall's gift, when Daddy decided to have all the members of the family chest X-rayed. Then it was discovered that I had had tuberculosis but that the condition had been completely healed.

I am now twenty-five years old, employed as a secretary, and enjoying good health.

(Signed) J. B.

We are writing this testimonial at the suggestion of Mrs. Ambrose Worrall and Rev. Robert Kirkley who conduct the New Life Clinic at the Mount Washington Methodist Church here in Baltimore.

Since March 1963 at which time I was told by my doctor that I would have to undergo a radical breast operation, my husband and I have attended these meetings. After the operation I was told by my surgeon that the operation was entirely successful and that I would not have to take any further treatment. However during December 1963 and January 1964 I began to suffer pains in my back. I consulted our family doctor, and he ordered X-ray pictures, knowing my previous medical history. The X-rays showed that my right lung was filled with fluid so he ordered me to the hospital for a thorough checkup. At the conclusion of this checkup it was determined that there was a malignancy in the plural wall of my right lung, the same side on which the radical was performed. We were told that this type of malignancy was inoperable and that my only hope was to retard its progress.

Since we had been attending the New Life Clinic meetings and knowing the wonderful miracles Our Lord was able to perform, we decided that here was our greatest hope for my ultimate recovery. We also decided to take advantage of any and all medical science available. This we did, attending meetings regularly and praying, knowing all the time that our prayers would be answered. My doctor from time to time ordered additional X-rays and just this past week after I had another X-ray he read the radiologist's report that my lung was entirely clear and no evidence of my previous affliction. He seemed entirely at a loss for words to explain this but we both have the answer. We shall be eternally grateful to our Lord and Savior and to Mrs. Worrall and Brother Kirkley for their help.

> (Signed) May and Herb Bosley
> Baltimore, Maryland

The following letter was published in He Is Able, *a magazine dealing with spiritual healing. It appears here with the permission of the magazine and the letter writer.*

June 8, 1962

Editor
He Is Able

Dear Sir:

I have been requested to write up for *He Is Able* a documentary of a personal healing which I received by the laying on of hands. On January 18, 1962 my children and I were badly burned by a flash fire at our cottage (a retreat place away from home). To relate the story of the healing itself, I must tell the chain of events following the terrible moment of tragedy.

An explosion completely engulfed my children and me in a furnace of fire. In one moment, in the twinkling of an eye, we were facing death. I scooped my children into my arms to try to smother the flames. In the void of this terrible moment, I thought we would perish but an amazing sequence followed. The fear vanished and a great flow of spiritual power surged through me as a gentle breeze in the springtime. A friend who was with us grabbed the youngest child from my arms and began to put out the blaze. His own clothing was charred so badly that it later fell apart, but he himself was not burned. Later he walked to a nearby farm house to get help to take us to the hospital in Gettysburg, Pennsylvania.

While he was gone, the children and I were as alone as any human beings can be. I called out for God and He filled our needs so wonderfully that it is scarcely believable. Without the presence of God, we could not have kept back the panic and shock which would have destroyed us. "His presence came like sunshine, like a glory in the breast." Now the peculiar nature of this experience was that God came in three persons. I have experienced the Holy Spirit, the presence of Jesus, and the nearness of the Father but never before in my experience as a Christian had I ever experienced the completeness of God in a convergence of the three distinct persons of the Trinity. The only analogy that I can find to describe this unusual experience is that it is the same sensation that a patient under certain types of anesthesia would experience on an operating table. He feels no pain but is perfectly aware of the presence of the surgeon and his staff and is able to comprehend the conversations between the surgeon and his staff without any concern. This is precisely what I experienced. God the Father was seen as with arms reclining on an arm rest from which proceeded all gifts of healing, of service, of love, ad infinitum. Jesus was seen as the bestower of these gifts, the Divine Physician. The Holy Spirit was seen as the instrument of God's will and purpose, preparing us for His Healing. Perhaps, the Holy Spirit might be analogous to the anesthetist. In any case, these three persons were in conversation, and I knew the subject of their conversation was how to preserve our lives and administer to our needs. At once, I realized the real danger we were in. At the same time, I knew that all I should do was to trust and to convey this trusting love to my children. Their response was beyond belief. If anyone thinks this is incredible, the promise of such a manifestation of God is found in John 14:23—"If a man loves me, he will keep my word, and my Father will love him, and we will come to him and make our home with him." Jesus does not mention the Holy Spirit in this verse, but does mention him in the 26th verse. Furthermore, the peace that He promised does come through Divine Visitation and acceptance of His love.

One week later at Maryland General Hospital, we were visited by the Rev. Jim Shannon and Mrs. Olga Worrall. At our request they came to pray for our healing and for the laying on of hands to effect the healing. One may think that this was anti-climactic. If God had already begun the healing, was it necessary to have the laying on of hands? The experience must speak for itself. God had delivered us from the fiery furnace, true; but there were further needful ministrations by the Medical Staff and by the Praying staff. Mrs. Worrall, Jim Shannon, Fran Creeden and several other consecrated Christians were the corps of the praying staff. When Mrs. Worrall visited me, my face was a mass of burnt skin of second and third degree burns. My hands were burnt so badly that they were hardly recognizable as hands. They were thickly and heavily bandaged. Under Mrs. Worrall's hands, I felt a delicious coolness like a balm swathing my hands. It was like liquid ice. Finding one spot at the very top of my head to place her hands, Mrs. Worrall prayed and the color began to shine through the mask of charred skin. Improvement and a consequent return to health was very rapid. The children too have been healed.

There are several reasons why I believe the laying on of hands was a catalyst in the healing of our bodies:

1. After the healing of the lepers, one returned to express his gratitude to Jesus. Jesus accepted this as a glorification of God, and then told the healed leper to show himself to the priests as the law required, that he might be declared clean. The permanent effects of any healing depends upon the use we make of our lives after healing, and that we give God the glory. It is a means of glorifying God. (Luke 17:11–19)

2. Also the healing of the blind man who had been blind from his birth was for the glorification of God. This formerly blind man gave a great witness to Jesus at his interrogation by the Pharisees. (John 9:1–41)

3. The laying on of hands is an act like baptism, which is for the outward manifestation of an inward state that has already been effected. It is fitting to fulfill all righteousness. (Matthew 3:13–15)

In conclusion, I will state what this "healing" means to me. It is the manifestation of the gospel, and that I might unashamedly proclaim the gospel as the power of God for salvation to them who have faith. Further, "I want you to know, brethren, that what has happened to me has really served to advance the gospel, so that it has become known throughout the whole (congregation whom I serve) and to all the rest (among my acquaintances) that my (burns and subsequent healing are) for Christ; and most of the brethren have been made confident in the Lord because of (this), and are much more bold to speak the word of God without fear. (Philippians 1:12–14)

> Sincerely yours,
> (Signed) Daniel G. Stone

January 16, 1965

Dear Mr. and Mrs. Worrall,

I wish to thank you both very much for the help you extended to Jack L. who is the younger brother of a young lady with whom I keep company, to use an old-fashioned phrase.

Two weeks ago today, Jack and a friend of his were repairing an automobile the friend owns. They had various automobile parts in gasoline. And as they carried these parts down a stairway, the friend stumbled, the gasoline spilled, and the entire stairway went up in flames. Jack, who was in the rear, suffered second degree burns of face and hands.

The following Tuesday night, you'll remember, I had mother call you. That very day, the doctor had indicated he might have to give Jack skin grafts, and some measure of disfigurement seemed quite possible. Almost needless to say, the L.'s were in despair—all the more so, because Jack is an only son whose father died six or seven years ago.

But within 24 hours, he began to show marked improvement. By Thursday, the doctor virtually assured him he would not have to employ skin grafts. And last Saturday, the doctor let him go home. Yesterday, Jack was assured he would suffer from no scars whatsoever.

Although they knew next to nothing about it, Jack's mother and sister were not adverse to the idea of spiritual healing and read your pamphlet thereon with considerable interest. I know they give you some of the credit. I give you just about all.

Jack, unfortunately, refused even to discuss the subject of spiritual healing with his sister. But then, he is only 20. And perhaps time will help open his eyes.

Again, many, many thanks. Perhaps you can use this little case history in one of your pamphlets or in some other way.

Sincerely,
(Signed) Hugh
(Hugh C. Sherwood)

P.S. This afternoon, it was brought to my attention that Jack's friend, Alan, had suffered a relapse and been transferred from a semi-private to a private room in the Greenwich, Conn. hospital. Alan was burned about the legs and at first it was not thought he was as badly burned as Jack. But he has not recovered as rapidly—and now this! We would appreciate it very much if you could extend your aid to him, too.

January 25, 1965

Dear Mr. Ambrose A. Worrall,

As you know I am a friend of Hugh Sherwood and his family. When Hugh asked me if I had heard of spiritual healing, I told him yes, but that I did not understand or know much about such healing. His second question was: do you and your family believe in God, my answer again was to the affirmative.

Shortly, thereafter, the call was made to your home, from that day a change began to take place with my brother's burns.

My brother John was burned with gasoline, receiving first, second and slight third degree burns on his face and hands. After Wednesday January sixth, our doctor told us that John was healing very quickly. Until this day, Dr. S. had told us very little and that John could possibly have skin grafting about the nose and lips.

On Friday, January 8th, this same doctor told us that John's recovery was remarkable and that he had nothing to do with his fast healing and that he had expected scarring.

It is now three weeks ago that John was burned and his face is clear, almost as if hands had wiped his face clear.

Mr. Worrall, John, my mother and I can never thank you enough for your help in John's complete recovery, but I will always believe and speak of this philosophy whenever I deem it correct.

Again thank you, with my deepest gratitude, I am sincerely,

(Signed) J. I. L.

৯ Appendix B

The following letter is one that we have sent out to hundreds of those who write to us asking for help:

Dear Friend:

Articles on healing in publications both in America and abroad have brought a great deluge of correspondence to us, requesting aid for the sick and suffering in all parts of the world.

The requests come from people of many faiths and races. There is but one God, and we make no attempt to convert people from their chosen religious affiliation. We seek only to give them confidence in the Divine Power that can restore wholeness of mind, body, and spirit.

There are many names given to this manifestation, such as faith healing, New Thought Healing, Spiritual Healing, etc.; but no matter what name may be chosen, we know that the power of God is available and is capable of restoring health, and improving conditions relative to peace and prosperity.

We know that this power is able to operate at a distance, therefore it is not necessary to arrange for a physical contact between the patient and the healer. It would not be possible for us to meet personally with the thousands of people who have written to us; but we can and will join with all who desire in five minutes of spiritual communion with the Divine Presence, from 9 P.M. to 9:05 P.M. every night on Eastern Standard Time (or Daylight Saving Time when in effect).

To those who co-operate with us in this plan, we ask that prayer, either aloud or in silence, be prayed immediately before 9 P.M., and then, at that hour, all praying cease, and that conscious awareness of the Divine Presence be sought for the five minutes by anticipating in expectancy some revelation, by intuition or sensing, of the actual demonstration of Divine Power.

It is important to co-operate with your doctor, and to regularly give thanks in your chosen place of worship.

We appreciate the thoughtfulness of those who send a stamped, self-addressed envelope.

Cordially yours,
(Signed) Mr. and Mrs. Ambrose A. Worrall